BECOMING A BRILLIANT TRAINER

A Teacher's Guide to Running Sessions and Engaging Learners

Alan Denton and Simon Brownhill

Routledge
Taylor & Francis Group

LONDON AND NEW YORK

First published 2018
by Routledge
2 Park Square, Milton Park, Abingdon, Oxon OX14 4RN

and by Routledge
711 Third Avenue, New York, NY 10017

Routledge is an imprint of the Taylor & Francis Group, an informa business

British Library Cataloguing in Publication Data
A catalogue record for this book is available from the British Library

Library of Congress Cataloging in Publication Data
Names: Denton, Alan, author. | Brownhill, Simon, author.
Title: Becoming a brilliant trainer : a teacher's guide to running sessions
and engaging learners / Alan Denton and Simon Brownhill.
Description: Abingdon, Oxon ; New York, NY : Routledge, 2018. | Includes
bibliographical references.
Identifiers: LCCN 2017021420 (print) | LCCN 2017045016 (ebook) | ISBN
9781315627960 (ebook) | ISBN 9781138645752 (hardback) | ISBN 9781138645769
(pbk.) | ISBN 9781315627960 (ebk)
Subjects: LCSH: Teachers--In-service training. | Professional learning
communities. | Teachers--Professional relationships.
Classification: LCC LB1731 (ebook) | LCC LB1731 .D44 2018 (print) | DDC
371.102--dc23
LC record available at https://lccn.loc.gov/2017021420

ISBN: 978-1-138-64575-2 (hbk)
ISBN: 978-1-138-64576-9 (pbk)
ISBN: 978-1-315-62796-0 (ebk)

Typeset in Interstate
by Fish Books Ltd.
Printed and bound by CPI Group (UK) Ltd, Croydon, CR0 4YY

BECOMING A BRILLIANT TRAINER

This essential guide provides both new and established trainers with accessible, innovative and engaging strategies to create an inspirational learning environment. This professional book is suitable for early years, primary and secondary teachers, school leaders and heads of department who are supporting their teaching colleagues in schools and other educational settings. It offers practical advice on planning and delivering great training sessions, including suggestions on how best to share existing knowledge in a group, and how to combine dialogue and written text to effectively develop ideas in the classroom.

The thinking behind each idea is not only clearly explained but is accompanied with a wealth of practical strategies that can be applied to a variety of training and teaching situations. This accessible resource is designed to help busy teaching professionals motivate their colleagues and deliver effective training. Generously illustrated throughout, the book is separated into four learning phases:

- preparing for successful training;
- offering direct input through new ideas;
- embedding the learning and developing the participant; and
- monitoring, evaluating and planning for the future.

Becoming a Brilliant Trainer will be an invaluable text for both trainee and qualified teachers, school leaders and all those with an interest in delivering great training sessions.

Alan Denton is a science-specialist teacher trainer working for schools, universities, the Science Learning Network and the Institute of Physics throughout East Anglia and further afield.

Simon Brownhill is Senior Teaching Associate in the Faculty of Education, University of Cambridge, UK.

For Ali Redmore who started me on this path,
and Ali Denton who keeps me going
AD

For Pop and Wilf
SPB

CONTENTS

PREFACE

The difficulty in writing a book like this is that we know there is no 'one-size-fits-all' for every training or teaching situation. This is also the joy of being a trainer, because it gives us a daily challenge and provides us with variety and an impetus to innovate and improve. If there were techniques that worked all the time for every type of situation then training would be an easy, repetitive job, and everyone would be equally excellent at it. Activities that work really well in one situation will be inappropriate for another; understanding why that is the case is crucial to running training that is successful. When discussing a range of activities for training, it therefore makes sense to look at research alongside our own observations to understand why these techniques work and when to use them.

Let us make two assumptions:

- Millions of people are expected to run training every year, either every day or occasionally.
- To excel as a trainer, you just need to have two attributes: great subject knowledge, and the skills to teach others!

Depending on what topic is the focus of your training, developing the required subject knowledge may take months, years or even decades to master. Sorry, but this book will not help you become an expert on the Spanish Inquisition, phonics, rocket science or any other fascinating topic. This book is also not designed to be the total guide to staff development, which can be a multi-faceted beast that includes coaching, mentoring, reviews, staff evaluation and many other techniques. But it should help you to teach your knowledge and skills to others, and it will help to innovate and improve any training that you run, whether these are one-hour sessions or an extensive programme lasting a year or longer.

If you are a teacher who has been asked to run teacher training then this book should also help you make the shift from teaching children to teaching adults (see Snapshot L for an introduction to the differences between teaching adults and children). You may be running training on a number of different topics: subject knowledge, subject-specific teaching techniques, creating conditions for learning, learning and teaching models, or more general teaching skills and techniques. You may be working with initial teacher trainees or with much more experienced teachers, and your teachers may themselves be working with 4-year-olds or 18-year-olds! Therefore, whilst we give you a range of options to consider when planning, running and assessing your training, and some activities that may be adapted to your teaching context, we do not give a prescriptive list of 'use this activity to teach this'.

We both have backgrounds in teaching, although these are very different: Simon started as an arts-loving early years primary school teacher, and Alan began teaching science and physics at a secondary school. We both still teach as our day jobs but we now teach adults, delivering training to other teachers and school leaders all over the UK and abroad. Between us we teach and lead hundreds of days of training for adults each year, both for those that have just started teaching and those that have been doing it a long time.

The switch from teaching children to teaching adults is not as straightforward as it may first sound. There are significant differences that teachers have to adapt to, arising from such things as the variations in adult temperament and learning styles, more complex relationships between trainers and adults, and the much more fleeting interactions trainers often have with their participants compared to the weekly lessons that school teachers have with their pupils.

Some of our best sessions happen as a result of planning our training collaboratively with one or more colleagues. This book is a glimpse into some of those meetings, the countless other discussions we have had with trainers that we have observed and supported over the years, and the many wonderful trainers that have mentored us along the way. We list many new (and established) activities that can add variety and interest into your training sessions, but each chapter also explains why we should be training in a specific way.

The book organisation should match how you plan your training sessions. We begin by looking at pre-course interaction that helps to inform your planning. We then explore many strategies for the training itself, such as direct teaching and working with text, before offering follow-up ideas to ensure that the training has a lasting impact.

Each chapter begins with an introduction highlighting some of the educational research into the topic covered. The style is designed to be easy to read, with any necessary academic terms explained as required so that the reader can look in more depth if they choose to. The book then calls on Alan and Simon's years of training and presents a large number of activities that have been used by them both. On each double-page spread one main idea is explored in depth informed by the theory. Some other ideas for activities are listed alongside as alternatives or as a next step. Knowing why an activity is effective relies on an understanding of how people learn; bearing this information in mind should help the reader to adapt and enhance the many ideas for their particular training situation without losing the benefits.

Snapshots, which are interspersed throughout the book, are pieces of practical advice from us and others that can have an impact on your whole training outlook; these include how to set up your training room (Snapshot A, Learning spaces, page 17) to how you can motivate adult learners (Snapshot H, Motivating adult learners, page 129).

When looking at the activities we encourage you to change them, break them, twist them and make them your own. Although we make suggestions about when you might use an activity in your training and how long it may take, do not follow this too rigidly. We will sometimes use one of our starters as the final task and other times we will take a 10-minute activity and run it for an hour. Be tempted to innovate and to try something new. We want trainers with all levels of experience to feel empowered to experiment so they can refresh and energise their training. Just remember to keep asking yourself beforehand why you are doing the activity, and afterwards if it was successful and why.

Good training does not come about by simply reading a book but by trying a range of teaching techniques and reflecting upon which are the most successful in any given situation, and learning to adjust your future teaching accordingly. We hope that we have been successful in creating a book that gives you the language, structure and background to help you to iteratively improve your training, and that will provide enough ideas to make it worth coming back to again and again. If we have succeeded, then it is the book we wish we had had before we got into this training game!

Alan Denton and Simon Brownhill

ACKNOWLEDGEMENTS

It is with the most heartfelt thanks that the following people are recognised:

Fay Turner and Elaine Wilson for the amazing opportunity to work on the Center of Excellence programme. Thanks also to all of our colleagues from the University of Cambridge that we collaborated with to deliver the energised 'Train the Trainers' training. To all of the trainers, co-trainers, interpreters, administrators, senior management and teachers that we have had the honour of working with and supporting in Kazakhstan – a massive thank you. To the Bolashak scholars (2016–17) who have willingly engaged in 'test runs' of different ideas we have developed for this book – cheers!

James de Winter for his tireless mentoring, friendship and wisdom, and Ali Redmore for her inspirational introduction into staff professional development, and the countless opportunities they and others have provided through the Centre for STEM Education, University of Hertfordshire. All teaching colleagues that work for or with the Science Learning Network – thank you.

All at Routledge, especially Sarah Richardson and Jillian Morrison for 'taking us on' and putting us in print. Damian Penfold for thoroughly cleaning up our text, plus Karl Harrington from Fish Books who helped deliver the final look and feel we were after.

Thank you all very much indeed.

INTRODUCTION

When we plan our training, we often begin by writing the questions we want participants to be able to answer at the end of it. Therefore, we have planned our introduction by asking ourselves the questions that we want this book to answer. With enough confidence, anyone can go into a room and 'run some training', if we mean they can stand up and talk for a while on something they know about.

So, what makes some training really stand apart from others?

There are lots of desirable characteristics that can make training feel special: having a knowledgeable and approachable trainer will help put people at ease; being memorable and fun may get good feedback from participants; well-organised resources and materials will make for a smoother experience. But these characteristics by themselves do not tell us if the training is successful.

So, what should great training look like to an observer looking in on the group?

During great training the new skills or knowledge being taught will be retained by the participants, and ultimately a change (for the better) will come about as a result of the training.

How can we ensure that new skills or knowledge are being taught and then retained by the participants?

Aims before activities is a term we introduce in Snapshot B, Planning, to explain that no matter what you are doing in a training session, it is crucial that you, as the trainer, first know why you are doing it. If we do not plan our training in this way there is a danger that the training will miss its mark and we will miss important learning opportunities.

For readers of a certain age who grew up with *Karate Kid*, or those of you that have a soft-spot for 80s movies, you may remember the scene in which Daniel-san has a tantrum because he thinks Mr Miyagi has been using him to do household chores rather than teach him karate. Mr Miyagi shows him that repeated sanding, waxing and painting has improved Daniel-san's fighting by strengthening his arm movements. Mr Miyagi clearly understood his aims and chose suitable, if unlikely, activities to match (don't worry – we won't be advocating any of these activities to strengthen your training!).

In your training you should create aims based upon your own experience, but also by taking the time to ask the participants what they want to achieve from the training before your training even begins (see Chapter 1, Pre-course engagement, page 6). Ideally your aims should be shared with the participants before arrival.

An important way to ensure that your training is working is by frequent assessment. An old teacher joke goes something like this:

> Someone boasts, 'I taught my cat to play flute.'
>
> A painful silence ensues. The cat does nothing.
>
> 'I said I taught him. I didn't say he learned to play.'

Without assessment we have no idea how successful our training is and when/whether we should move onto the next activity/input. Whilst assessment does not have to be intrusive or look like a test, it is important that we include assessment in any good training, with many even arguing that assessment should be considered before you even plan your teaching activities (Wiggins and McTighe, 2005). A high proportion of the activities in this book give opportunities for the trainer to assess how the participants are progressing during the training itself, to enable training sessions to be responsive to individual needs. An in-depth look at how we can assess at the end of a course is discussed in Chapter 11, Assessment.

We believe one of the most important techniques in getting people to retain information is not only to practice good revision techniques, but also to take time to explain what these techniques are and how they work. A summary of the most effective revision techniques is given in Snapshot K, Revision (page 177), based on the work by Dunlosky *et al.* (2013).

How can we ensure a change will come about as a result of the training?

The best thing you can do to encourage change as a result of your training is to plan for it (see Chapter 12, Making an impact). Allow time for participants to reflect upon your training and ask them to discuss how their learning will impact on them, and others, in the future. If participants are actively involved in planning for change, and can see how it will be positive for their work, then change is more likely to occur (Guskey, 2002).

So, how else can we improve our training?

The term **teaching chain** is introduced in Snapshot D, Teaching chains (page 63), to explain why some sessions have better pace and flow more easily than others. Often, a great learning activity does not exist by itself but as part of a series of linked activities that naturally lead into others, and these activities demonstrate increasing challenge and/or an increase in participant independence. Simple activities that can be used before or after each of the main activities to create teaching chains are given throughout the book; we do, however, encourage readers to develop their own.

In some ways, teaching adults can be easier than teaching children, but there are differences that need to be embraced for existing teachers. Knowles *et al.* (2012) explore in detail the importance of pitching your training at an appropriate level for adults, examples of which include being clear with your aims and how these can have an impact outside of the teaching room, providing problems with a sufficient challenge that are linked to real-world problems, giving them independence and taking into account their existing experience. We examine the motivations for adult learners in Snapshot H, Motivating adult learners (page 129).

When training we have to select strategies in response to the needs of our subject matter, our audience, the shape of the room we are in and even the time of day. It is possible just to open a book like this at random and choose a new strategy; whilst this can be innovative it is not necessarily informed innovation. You, as the expert, the trainer, and the person who knows your audience, will have to look at the complete picture of your situation before selecting the most suitable activities. The ideas explored in the Snapshots do not generally make suggestions about an activity to run, but instead offer a suite of considerations to be mindful of whilst you are leading them, such as how to run inclusive training (see Snapshot I, Inclusive training, page 145). Finally, if an activity you try does not work as well as planned, think about why it did not work in this situation and if it may be worth trying in another situation, or if it needs to be slightly altered. Being a reflective practitioner is what enables some trainers to get better and better with experience (Scales *et al.*, 2013).

Ideally, training courses should be conducted over a sustained period of time if they are to have a strong impact (DfE, 2016). Where this is not possible, and training is only for a short period of time (such as a single day), the training should have narrow, achievable aims.

To maximise the impact on our participants, we can see the need to extend our training before and beyond the 'classroom' itself; it should never just be about planning a few engaging activities. Our *A-frame of training* (Figure A, page 4) highlights the five key areas to increase the value of your training:

- **Aims** – What the training sets out to achieve for everyone, but also consideration of any individual's learning requirements for the course.
- **Activities** – A range of teaching ideas that are used to find out about the participants' existing knowledge, to transfer new knowledge or skills, or to consolidate and embed this new learning.
- **Assessment** – Planned alongside the activities, assessment does not need to be intrusive but should enable the participants and the trainer to personalise and improve the experience during the training course.
- **Action plan** – Participants should develop an action plan as a result of your training (hopefully on the day itself), and they are then responsible for ensuring that they implement these changes when they have finished.
- **After-care** – Participants should be fully supported after the course by their organisation, managers and peers, and possibly by you as their trainer. They should be asked to review the impact that their training has had on them and others around them. The training should provide high-quality materials/weblinks to extend their learning, and any tasks they are asked to complete should be meaningful.

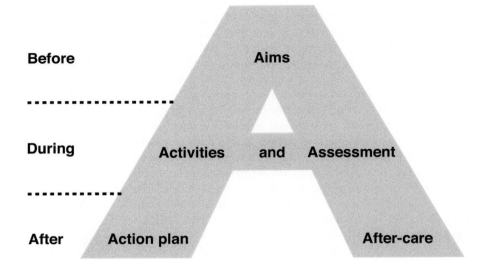

Before

Aims

During

Activities   **and**   **Assessment**

After   **Action plan**   **After-care**

FIGURE A The *A-frame of training*: getting the most from any training situation

> **NOTE!**
> **At the time of writing all of the tinyurl.com links offered in this book were active.**
> **As information on the internet is regularly changed, updated or removed, it is**
> **anticipated that some links may not work for the reader. The authors apologise**
> **for this, but it is hoped that readers will recognise that this is out of the authors'**
> **control.**

References

DfE (2016). *Standard for Teachers' Professional Development*. Available at: www.gov.uk/government/uploads/system/uploads/attachment_data/file/537031/160712_-_PD_Expert_Group_Guidance.pdf (accessed 18 November, 2016).

Dunlosky, J., Rawson, K., Marsh, E., Nathan, M. and Willingham, D. (2013). Improving students' learning with effective learning techniques: Promising directions from cognitive and educational psychology. *Psychological Science in the Public Interest*, 134(1), 4–58.

Guskey, T. R. (2002). Professional development and teacher change. *Teachers and Teaching*, 8(3), 381–391.

Knowles, M. S., Holton, E. F. and Swanson, R. A. (2011). *The Adult Learner*, 7th edn. Amsterdam: Elsevier.

Scales, P. (2013). *Teaching In The Lifelong Learning Sector*, 2nd edn. Maidenhead: Open University Press.

Wiggins, G. and McTighe, J. (2005). *Understanding by Design: Innovation*. Upper Saddle River, NJ: Prentice Hall/Alexandria, VA: Association for Supervision and Curriculum Development.

Learning phase 1

Preparing for successful training

Chapter 1

Pre-course engagement

Alan says:

❝ Most of the time, the reasons why a participant has come on your course match up neatly with what you are planning to do on your course, but sometimes they do not. On one memorable occasion, I just about snatched victory from the jaws of defeat when I realised the course that had been advertised was really quite different from the course I had been asked to teach! Fortunately, on this occasion I practiced what I preached and every participant had been asked to write down what they wanted from the course before they arrived – by reading through these in the morning I was able to work out that there had been a misunderstanding and I rapidly re-planned what we were doing. Although the resultant day was not quite the course I would have planned, it worked: I was able to steer discussions a different way, alter some examples, and change the emphasis of the sessions – everyone left happy. I created a new rule that day, which is that I want to be copied in to the emails the participants receive! ❞

It is mid-morning and you are checking your emails as you sip a nice cup of coffee. One email intrigues you. You click it open ...

Coffee SPRAYS out of your mouth, all over the kitchen table!

'OH NO!'

OH YES!

You've been given some pre-course tasks to do before you attend that training you are going on next week!

Whether or not this is you, in reality there are participants who will react negatively to being asked to undertake pre-course activities associated with your training. Part of this chapter introduction considers the various reasons for this and suggests ways through which this might be positively addressed. To begin with, we set out to clarify what is actually meant by 'pre-course engagement', what it means for participants and trainers, why pre-course engagement is considered to be important, and what kinds of activity can be used by trainers to engage participants before 'Training Day'!

Pre-course engagement – what do you mean?

Pre-course engagement refers to any activity that gets participants 'ready' for the training they are booked on. By this, we mean the sharing of relevant information before participants attend your training, along with the undertaking of purposeful tasks that are linked to the training focus.

What does this mean for participants?

Quite simply this means participants doing something! This can range from them reading or writing, to undertaking a practical task. We present a selection of quality pre-course activities later on in this chapter introduction, but first we highlight that pre-course engagement for participants means actively engaging with something, be it an electronic information text, an online video or a paper-based questionnaire.

> **NOTE!**
> **You do not always have to set participants a pre-course task, especially if it is not going to improve their learning. For a single day's training, however, we consider it to be very important to set pre-course tasks due to the time constraints on covering all of the subject content.**

What does pre-course engagement mean for trainers?

Pre-course engagement for trainers also means doing something! This involves the preparation of pre-course materials that are sent out to participants in an electronic or paper-based format. Some trainers argue that this is just 'extra work' and so choose not to make pre-course engagement an integral part of their training – we strongly oppose this: it can play a very important first step in broadening the reach of your training, and ultimately increasing the overall impact. Once relevant materials have been prepared electronically, they may be adaptable for other training that you deliver, dependent (naturally) on the training focus. There are, of course, other reasons why we feel pre-course engagement is important:

- It helps participants get the most out of the training you offer.
- It sets an expectation that your training is about learning, not just 'a day off work'.
- It gets participants to start thinking about the training focus so that they do not come to it 'cold' on the day.
- It allows you to pack as much training as possible into the time available.

The importance of pre-course materials cannot be underestimated either: Bradbury (2014) argues that '[a]s well as providing people with the necessary logistical information, pre-course materials tell people what to expect and what the benefits of attending will be. They can also let people know about any pre-course preparation they need to complete, along with anything they need to bring.' Well-prepared pre-course materials can therefore help to deal effectively with the 'excitement, anxiety, and fear' (Conrad, 2002: 205) that participants are likely to feel prior to attending your training by offering them:

- clear aims, objectives and outcomes
- a concise description of the training
- essential 'logistical information' that is often overlooked (see Table 1.1).

Sharing this information with participants is a crucial part of pre-course engagement – this can be included in the email sent to participants that signposts them to pre-course activities you would like them to engage with, or it can be summarised as part of an introductory letter. But this begs an important question: how do you 'engage' participants in these pre-course activities?

We know from personal experience that professionals are busy people, and asking them to undertake pre-course tasks can be a 'big ask'. Work pressures, family commitments, time

Table 1.1 Essential information to share before the training with participants

- The title of the training event
- The date(s) of the training
- Start and finishing times including breaks
- The location where the training is taking place, e.g. the name of the building, the specific room, the full address and postcode
- Travel directions to the training location
- Parking arrangements
- Arrangements for refreshments and any meals
- The name of the trainer (very important!)
- Contact details – phone numbers/email addresses of the trainer and/or administrative support, and the best telephone number for the day in case they are lost or late

constraints, sufficient access to resources, and motivation/energy levels are all influencing factors that can result in some participants turning up to training sessions 'having not done their homework'! McCall and Young (2010: 2) suggest that there are six broad categories (or 'considerations') to make pre-course activities 'compelling, enjoyable and productive'. We explore five relevant considerations in Table 1.2 that positively address some of the factors identified above.

Of course, we cannot force participants to undertake pre-course activities. We can, however, use some little 'tricks of the trade' to actively assure that they will engage with them:

- Limit the number of pre-course activities you want participants to undertake. We suggest between one to three tasks.
- Remember that 'variety is the spice of life' – offer tasks to participants that get them choosing, researching, rank ordering, reading, reviewing, reflecting and evaluating.
- Give gentle email reminders (one week/three days before the training starts) as a way of usefully bringing the pre-course activities to the forefront of participants' minds!
- State that the first planned activity during the training session will be discussing a key pre-course task (this often seems to work as a way of getting them to do it!).
- Encourage participants to make a choice about the kind of evidence they would like to bring with them to show that they have engaged with the pre-course tasks set, e.g. pictures, photographs, videos, written notes, annotated slides, Prezi presentations, and/or print outs.

So, what activities can be given to participants as pre-course tasks?

Well, the list is endless! Here are just a few that we 'pick and choose' from for our own training:

- completing a questionnaire
- compiling an activity log
- exploring quality websites
- reading a professional article
- taking an online test
- formulating personal learning targets
- watching a TED Talks video
- researching a contemporary theory
- undertaking a subject knowledge audit
- drawing a diagram
- listing three key areas for professional development
- reviewing a passage of text
- preparing an informative poster

- creating a PowerPoint presentation
- annotating personal planning
- taking digital photographs
- reflecting on policy documents
- identifying effective strategies
- collecting workbook samples
- writing a 250-word essay

- editing an ineffective worksheet
- designing a quick quiz
- producing a 5-day pre-learning diary
- discussing provocative quotations by educationalists with colleagues in their place of work.

Table 1.2 Considerations when assigning pre-course tasks

No.	Consideration	Details and suggestions
1	Ensure pre-course tasks add value	Pre-course tasks should be seen as a 'gateway' to the content of the training session. - Make it clear to participants how the pre-course tasks contribute to the training content, the objectives/outcome, and their ability to participate in the actual training session. - Plan opportunities for participants to discuss and review these tasks throughout the training session so that they serve as an integral part of the training experience.
2	Create a sense of urgency	Participants may not get around to completing the tasks set because of other commitments. - Make sure you send out the tasks in plenty of time for participants to complete them – at least two weeks before the training date. - Offer each task an estimated completion time so that participants know how much time they should dedicate to it before starting. - Give participants a choice of tasks to complete, e.g. any two out of the four that are offered to them.
3	Provide incentives	Motivate participants by rewarding their engagement with the pre-course tasks. This could be in the form of verbal praise, visual acknowledgement (a smile, a wink) or tangible objects (pens, tokens, stickers). Recognition could be given individually or on a group/whole group basis.
4	Make it enjoyable	Pre-course tasks that engage participants will help to foster a receptive group. They should not be just 'fun' but more educationally stimulating by having a clear learning focus. - Avoid 'death-by-reading'. If only four paragraphs of the text are relevant then only include these in the reading, or highlight them as being of importance. - Promote reflective thinking by encouraging participants to 'look back' at their own practice in relation to the training focus.
5	Implement accountability	Establish a contract between you and your participants by explaining that you have designed meaningful pre-course tasks and will deliver a training session that meets stated objectives. In return, you expect them to 'uphold their end of the contract' by coming prepared to participate fully in the training session – this means they will have undertaken the pre-course tasks you have set them.

Adapted from McCall and Young (2010: 2)

In summary:

■ Good training engages participants before the training starts with useful information and pre-course activities.

■ Make sure pre-course materials are sent out to participants around two weeks before your first training session so that they have sufficient time to engage with the tasks set. If these are sent too early participants will delay starting, and if they are sent too late they may not have time to complete them.

■ The tone of the pre-course materials sets the tone for the training you deliver – make the materials warm, friendly and inviting. Always check that there are no spelling, grammar or punctuation errors.

■ The best pre-course tasks are meaningful, directly linked to the training focus, do not take too long to complete, and are actually used in the training session.

Table 1.3 Recommended readings and resources

Source	Title	Author/s	Year	Web link
Training Guide	Training Guide and Training Techniques: I. Pre-training Activities (to do before training) (pp. 2–9)	UNESCO	2004	http://tinyurl.com/la89jy2
PDF	6 Ways to Make Pre-Work Compelling	McCall and Young	2010	http://tinyurl.com/y932maa7
Web column	Brain Science: Pre-training Is Essential to a Complete Training Package	Kohn	2014	http://tinyurl.com/ya9sj8ab

Personalised learning aims

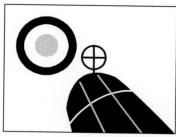

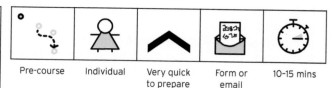

| Pre-course | Individual | Very quick to prepare | Form or email | 10–15 mins |

Offer participants a chance to influence the content of the training by encouraging them to write what the most important aims for the session(s) are going to be for them. Try using a simple form with enough space for participants to write in. Where possible these should be emailed or posted out to participants in advance so that you receive thoughtful responses. Questions can be directed at the participants directly, e.g. 'What do you hope to get out of this course (e.g. knowledge, experience, skills, and attitudes)?' However, questions can also be targeted more widely, e.g. 'How could this training help others you work with?'

Benefits
- Many personalised learning aims you read will not alter or affect your training as they will match what you were going to do anyway, but frequently they will identify an idea that is key for particular participants.

Considerations
- You may want to remind participants of your planned aims before they fill in their form ...
- ... or you may not if you want to be more responsive to their needs.

Set-up tips
- If possible, ask participants to send their personalised learning aims back to you in advance of the training. If you can read them before the session(s) then you can more easily alter and adjust your input, planned activities and timings.
- If participants bring their personalised learning aims on the day of the actual training, plan a short activity that they can complete without your intervention, so that you have time to read their aims. Or just collect their aims whilst they are having coffee before the start of the session.

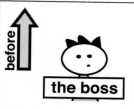

On the form encourage participants to discuss their personalised learning aims with their line manager (or equivalent). If appropriate, you could ask for the line manager's signature and email address.

Ask participants to compare their personalised learning aims with each other to see what the similarities and differences are (and to allow you time to read them too).

Although it is time intensive, it can be very valuable to discuss participant's aims with them individually in person.

Highlight the learning aims

If the training course has got a large number of learning aims (perhaps because it is a multi-day course, or it links directly to a legal framework, for example), it can be worth sharing all the aims in advance with participants so that they can understand what the whole course entails. Before they arrive, participants could be asked to reflect on how confident they are against each of the aims, perhaps by 'RAG' rating themselves using coloured dots (marking each point as **r**ed if they are unhappy, **a**mber if they are unsure or **g**reen if they are confident).

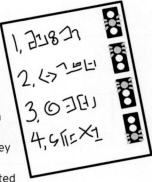

Extension – Ask participants to look at each other's 'RAG' rated learning aims to see what the main challenges will be, and what you should not waste time covering in depth.

Quiz 'em

To make a formal assessment of participant knowledge/ skills, a good idea is to give out a diagnostic quiz before the training. This will give you and the participants a base-level assessment, which can help you to ensure that the pace of delivery is suitable and that support is targeted at the appropriate topics. A range of questions can be used – multiple-choice, simple answers or more in-depth written questions. You should be confident that participants have taken the time to fill this in (and that they have completed it themselves!). You should also ensure that the results of the quiz are used during the session or else it will seem like a waste of their time.

Alternative – Give quizzes out on arrival to discourage cheating.

Show and tell

When it is appropriate, participants can be asked to bring along some of their work to use as a discussion point on the day. This may be something they have previously written, built, created or done, or something the participants have supported others to do (for example, educators may be asked to bring along students' work). If the work itself is not easily portable, photos or scanned images could be brought in as evidence.

Alternative – Tell participants in advance that they may be asked to speak about a specific example of something they have previously done well (or not so well).

Writing your own success

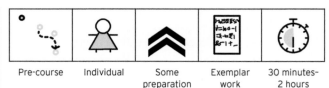

| Pre-course | Individual | Some preparation needed | Exemplar work | 30 minutes– 2 hours |

Sometimes it may be appropriate to ask participants to prepare something written in advance specifically for the training. As this may be a substantial amount of work for the participants, it is often more appropriate to seek this for courses where they are receiving some kind of certification, accreditation or professional recognition at the end. There are a wide range of evidence sources that may apply here, but it could be a log-book that records instances that the participant has performed an activity, writing an account of something they have done well or an analysis of a situation they have had to deal with that has been challenging on some level.

Benefits
- This can be a very good way of understanding the 'lived experience' of participants before they arrive on the training; it also encourages them to reflect on their own practice.

Considerations
- Even if success on the course can only be achieved by completing this task, it is still worth acknowledging the amount of work that has gone into compiling the evidence.
- Equally, if something is found lacking in the participant's work, then you can support them to address this, but you also may be able to ask other participants to share their work and offer peer support.

Set-up tips
- It is often beneficial to send out some exemplar work, so that participants can clearly see your expectations (make sure this is suitably anonymised).

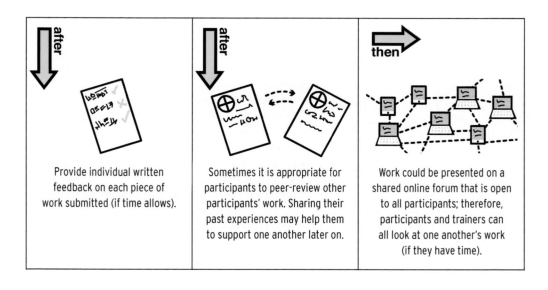

Provide individual written feedback on each piece of work submitted (if time allows).

Sometimes it is appropriate for participants to peer-review other participants' work. Sharing their past experiences may help them to support one another later on.

Work could be presented on a shared online forum that is open to all participants; therefore, participants and trainers can all look at one another's work (if they have time).

Reading your own success

When sending around required readings before a training course, it is more likely to be thought about in depth by participants if they are given an activity to undertake whilst they are reading it. For example, if they are reading a long piece written by the trainer or others, participants could simply be asked to summarise the five key points from the reading, or to highlight anything that they found surprising. Equally, you could send out some case studies or scenarios relating to a situation that you need them to be able to discuss during the training. When sending around stimulus material for reading, be aware that some participants may not read it until the day (if at all). If the reading does not matter, it may not be worth sending it out.

Deputy Dawg

Rather than doing all the hard work yourself on the day, try deputising to some (or all) of the participants in advance by giving them a special task to prepare for the training. This may be to plan to speak about something they have done or read, or to present about one of the learning aims you have chosen. You can choose the participants by potluck, but if you know them then you can select the right person for the task.

Alternative - If you have two tasks, you can send the first one to half of the participants and the other to the rest. On arrival, ask them to pair up to explain what they have read/done.

Data miner

There will be times when you can ask participants to bring some data with them for the course so that they can analyse it with their trainer's help and support. It may be that the participant already has easy access to the data and they just need to bring it with them. However, at times you may ask participants to collect a set of data, for example by asking participants to send around questionnaires to other staff members or relevant people.

Alternative - If you want everyone to bring the data in a uniform and comparable fashion, you will need to provide clear templates for questionnaires/ spreadsheets/etc.

32.4	98.1	423.0	1.1	0.4	78.8	21.7	1.	
87.4	180.0	27.7	69.7	123.8	96.4	78.2	14	
0	7.2	42.3	12.4	75.1	52.4	21.4	12.7	9.
9.0	37.4	97.1	91.9	76.8	45.0	9.9	3.3	31.1
1.8	3.7	35.7	32.3	88.4	91.4	37.9	128.8	21.7
37.5	314.7	3.6	17.4	77.2	32.4	23.0	12.4	1.7
37.4	12.5	753.4	2.1	120.1	74.1	0.4	108.8	97.1	3
2	57.8	3.0	127.4	82.0	49.2	42.4	32.4	14.2	124.2	57
2.4	65.5	12.8	8.1	64.5	87.7	12.4	12.7	23.5	912.4	65.5
12.7	377.8	32.4	98.1	423.0	1.1	0.4	78.8	21.7	12.7	377.8
14.8	11.1	87.4	180.0	27.7	69.7	123.8	96.4	78.2	14.8	11.1
1	9.4	425.0	7.2	42.3	12.4	75.1	52.4	21.4	12.7	9.4	425.0

References

Bradbury, A. (2014). Creating engaging pre-course materials. CIPD Learning ToolClicks, 24 March. Available at: www.cipd.co.uk/toolclicks/learning/training-tools/planning-designing-training/creating-engaging-materials/default.aspx (accessed 10 July, 2016).

Conrad, D. L. (2002). Engagement, excitement, anxiety and fear: Learners' experiences of starting an online course. *American Journal of Distance Education*, 16(4), 205–226.

McCall, D. and Young, J. (2010). 6 Ways to Make Pre-Work Compelling. Designing Productive Virtual Meetings Series. Facilitate.com. Available at: www.facilitate.com/support/facilitator-toolkit/docs/6-Ways-to-make-prework-compelling.pdf (accessed 29 June 2017).

UNESCO (2004). *Training Guide and Training Techniques*. Bangkok: UNESCO Asia and Pacific Regional Bureau for Education.

Snapshot A: Learning spaces

Good trainers recognise that the actual training they deliver only plays a small (but significant) part in whether it is deemed 'good' or 'useful' in the minds of participants – if there are no handouts then it is 'thumbs down'; if the lunch is poor then it is a 🙁 on the evaluation form! Interestingly, the space in which participants are trained also serves as a key factor to the perceived success of your training and what participants actually learn in it. In this Snapshot we briefly consider:

1   the basic components of an effective learning space;
2   different kinds of learning space that can be made for adults in a typical training room;
3   ways to maximise participant learning in the learning space.

These considerations will be explored through 'Research and practice' summaries (Table 1.4), drawing on research-based knowledge in the field and effective practical strategies for quality training provision.

> **NOTE!**
> **We recognise that there will be aspects of the learning space that you simply cannot control, e.g. the room in which you are asked to train, or the amount of space that is available within it. We offer these suggestions in the hope that you may be able to utilise some of these if/when the opportunity arises.**

Some room layouts that we regularly use are shown in Figure 1.1, alongside some of the advantages and disadvantages they have. We do not have a preferred layout but will set up the room based on what is required for that training session: we recommend that you do the same!

We offer a small collection of simple ideas to energise your thinking and enhance your practices associated with creating the optimum learning space for participants and your training. Again, these are simply suggestions which you can choose to use or not if you don't want to!

1   Ask participants how they would like the training room to be arranged at the start of the session/day – use this as an opportunity for participants to get to know one another as they work together to organise the learning space.
2   MacKeracher (2004: 190) asserts that '[l]earning can be adversely affected by ... poor air quality'. To that end, make sure that learning spaces are aired before and during the training (open the doors and windows, weather permitting), use an inexpensive plug-in air purifier, put plants on working tables, and encourage participants to 'Go get some fresh air!' during coffee breaks and lunchtimes.
3   Promote participant independence, interdependence and self-motivation by taking advantage of breakout spaces (other nearby rooms which are not being used) in the training building.
4   Cover vibrant and stimulating displays in the learning space with easel paper as they could distract participants from their learning.

5   Create innovative little learning spaces in the training room, e.g. make learning dens by throwing drapes over tables, turn tables on their sides to create learning forts, and hang fabric over string washing lines to create learning tents/canopies.

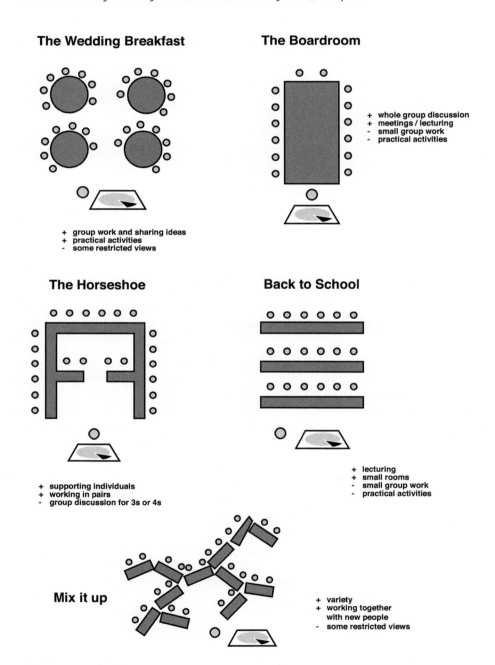

FIGURE 1.1 Our frequently used room layouts, with some of the advantages/disadvantages

Table 1.4 Techniques to improve learning spaces

Research and practice summary 1	*Learning spaces: the basics*
What is known	'[B]right, quiet, warm, safe, clean, comfortable and healthy environments are an important component of successful teaching and learning' (Barrett and Zhang, 2009: 2).
Implications for training and trainers	▪ Ensure you switch on the lights, open the curtains/blinds, 'crank up the thermostat' (but not too hot), and give the tables a quick wipe over if needed before your participants arrive. ▪ Play calming mood music (at a low volume) prior to the start of your training. ▪ Invest in some floor cable covers for health and safety reasons. ▪ Provide fresh water (flavours optional) on working tables, along with snacks like dried fruits or seeds so participants can 'Drink While They Think' and 'Nibble While They Scribble' (Brownhill, 2016: 10). ▪ Through pre-course communications, invite participants to bring their own seat cushions/pads from their workplace/home to support them when sitting.
Relevant research	Graetz (2006)
Research and practice summary 2	*Learning spaces for adults in the training room*
What is known	There are a range of possible learning spaces that you can use for 'various modes and group sizes' (Fisher, 2005: 2.03). Learners should be able to 'move around the various learning environments to suit the particular learning task' (p. 2.03) within the training room.
Implications for training and trainers	▪ Ensure that every participant has an individual pod (space) for them to sit at, think and work in the training room. ▪ Show participants how to *safely* rearrange tables and chairs to aid small group collaborative and cooperative learning. ▪ Promote the idea of activity-rich spaces by inviting participants to engage in activities on the floor (tables to the side of the room), on paper temporarily attached to the wall, on interactive white-boards or flipcharts, or at communal table-top spaces (with all of the tables put together). ▪ Encourage participants to make use of informal learning spaces around the training building, e.g. in corridors, the library or the cafeteria, under verandas and gazebos, and outdoor areas such as benches or the grass (provide blankets).
Relevant research	Radovan and Makovec (2015)
Research and practice summary 3	*Maximising participant learning in the learning space*
What is known	'Everyone has preferred learning environments ... Participants thrive in learning spaces which are compatible with their learning temperament [way of learning]' (Percy, 1989: 98).
Implications for training and trainers	▪ Consider using technology in your training to aid participants' learning, e.g. phones. ▪ Capitalise on the space offered outdoors (weather permitting) for participants to move, make music/noise and engage in purposeful drama/role play activity. Use indoor spaces for getting to know you and getting ready to learn activities – see Chapter 2, Getting to know you and getting ready to learn, for more details. ▪ Signpost/take participants to other relevant learning spaces in the local area, e.g. libraries, museums, art galleries, sports centres, parks and woods.
Relevant research	Kolb and Kolb (2005)

Table 1.5 Recommended readings and resources

Source	Title	Author/s	Year	Web link
Book	Creating Learning Spaces: Training and Professional Development for Trainers	Attwell and Baumgartl (eds)	2008	http://tinyurl.com/5koar9
Workshop cards	What If? ... Learning spaces workshop cards	Futurelab	2009	http://tinyurl.com/haxvswf

References

Barrett, P. and Zhang, Y. (2009). *SCRI Research Report 2: Optimal Learning Spaces - Design Implications for Primary Schools*. Salford: University of Salford. Available at: www.oecd.org/edu/innovation-education/centreforeffectivelearningenvironmentscele/43834191.pdf (accessed 26 December, 2015).

Brownhill, S. (2016). *Stimulating Story Writing! Inspiring Children Aged 7-11*. London: Routledge.

Fisher, K. (2005). *Linking Pedagogy and Space*. Proposed planning principles, Department of Education and Training, 16 March. Available at: www.education.vic.gov.au/Documents/school/principals/infrastructure/pedagogyspace.pdf (accessed 26 December, 2015).

Graetz, K. A. (2006). The psychology of learning environments. In: Oblinger, D. G. (ed.) *Learning Spaces*. Washington, DC: Educause (pp. 6.1-6.14). Available at: http://tinyurl.com/jq88pfw (accessed 13 September, 2017).

Kolb, A. Y. and Kolb, D. A. (2005). Learning styles and learning spaces: Enhancing experiential learning in higher education. *Academy of Management Learning & Education*, 4(2), 193-212.

MacKeracher, D. (2004). *Making Sense of Adult Learning*, 2nd edn. Toronto: University of Toronto Press.

Percy, D. (1989). *Adult Study Tactics: A Springboard to Learning*. South Yarra: Macmillan Education Australia.

Radovan, M. and Makovec, D. (2015). Adult learners' learning environment perceptions and satisfaction in formal education: Case study of four East-European countries. *International Education Studies*, 8(2), 101-112. Available at: files.eric.ed.gov/fulltext/EJ1060807.pdf (accessed 29 July, 2017).

Chapter 2

Getting to know you and getting ready to learn

> **Simon says:**
>
> " There is no doubt in my mind that good training facilitates time and space for you to get to know those attending your sessions, and for participants to get to know each other. There is nothing worse than participants sitting uncomfortably next to one another around a table or in straight rows with a 'sea of silence' in the air! I always find observing participants when they engage in getting to know you (GTKY) activities very 'telling' – you can tell who are the strong characters, those that are reserved or reflective, those who are just at the training to 'have a break' from the day job, and those who think they know it all – it is a bit like 'spotting' character types in the classroom! I always make a mental note of this information and use it to help me organise my groups, moving people around the room so that they do not dominate, coast or fall asleep! I have always enjoyed using getting ready to learn (GRTL) activities in my training because it helps to get participants in the right 'mind-set' – you are here to learn! I decided once to give select participants a chance to deliver a different GRTL activity to a small group at the same time – it was brilliant to see everyone engaged because there was nowhere for anyone to hide! Letting participants plan and lead GRTL activities at different times in the training day also helps to give me a five-minute breather – good training can be exhausting! "

Take a moment to ask yourself the following:

- When was the last time you were a participant at a training session?
- How did you feel when you entered the training room?
- Did you know anyone there?
- Did you introduce yourself to the trainer and other participants or did you wait for others to introduce themselves to you?

Based on our own experiences of being trained by others, we suspect many of you may have felt a bit diffident or slightly reserved, which are normal responses to this kind of situation. There are numerous reasons why participants coming to your training will react in a similar way, a selection of which is offered below:

- Personality traits – some participants are naturally shy and 'distant' when entering a new setting or meeting new people.
- Role reversal – those attending the training may be educators in their working role (i.e., teachers); now they are the learners (who are typically children/young people).
- Insecurity – participants may be apprehensive about the focus of the training if it is completely new to them or if they know very little about it.
- Sleepiness – those in attendance may feel sluggish at the start of the day/training session as a result of the demands of their professional/personal lives.

Being a good trainer means that not only are you aware of the reasoning offered above but you are able to positively address these considerations as they can impact on the success of the training you conduct. Sisco suggests that trainers should initially use training time to 'reduce tension and anxiety, help acquaint participants with each other ... and assist the instructor in getting to know class members and their range of experiences' (1991: 46). This can be achieved by:

- greeting participants informally;
- helping them to 'settle in', e.g. distributing badges, signposting them to where the toilets and refreshments are;
- asking and answering general questions;
- casually introducing them to their peers for the day.

These simple activities help to build professional relationships that not only positively contribute to the social environment but also establish a climate that is conducive for adult learning. Being able to 'put a name to a face' is particularly important as it helps participants to feel as if the training is being personalised to them. However, we believe that an effective training session starts before a training session begins! What we mean by this is that your work as a trainer starts when participants enter the training room and not when the clock strikes nine – those activities described above should thus be undertaken prior to the start of the actual training so that they do not 'eat' into valuable training time.

Getting to know you

Once all of your participants are in attendance and the training begins, good practice usually involves them engaging in some interactive 'getting acquainted' or getting to know you (GTKY) activities; these are particularly useful at the start of new training. Also known as icebreakers, these activities are used for the following reasons (adapted from Dunlap, 2013: 3):

- To encourage participants to relax.
- To support the formation of close bonds with their peers.
- To foster a sense of community within the training room/space.
- To help everyone feel comfortable in expressing their ideas in a safe learning environment.
- To energise participants in becoming more active in the learning process.

While icebreakers are typically engaging and exciting in nature, the benefits of using them can be countered by discomfort and tension that can be caused if trainers do not carefully select appropriate icebreakers, or participants see them as being irrelevant or poorly run. The result will be participants who are reluctant to engage with them, and the whole training getting off to a poor start. To ensure this does not happen, you are encouraged to be mindful of the following considerations (see Table 2.1) when choosing and using icebreakers, the most important of which is being clear about the purpose of the icebreaker, ensuring that partic-ipants are made aware of this verbally either before, during and/or after the activity.

It has been suggested '[t]oo often we see the same old icebreakers and energizers being used at training courses' (University of Manchester, n.d.: 2). In response to this, we offer you a selection of online resources that offer a wealth of fresh icebreakers for you to add to your metaphorical 'Trainer Toolkit' (see Table 2.2).

Table 2.1 Considerations and examples for trainers to be mindful of when choosing and using appropriate icebreakers

Consideration	Examples
Type	Introductory, GTKY, team building, topic exploration, 'excite and engage'
Purpose	Build trust and co-operation, initiate conversations and discussion, develop team building skills, linkage to the training focus, foster critical thought
Group size	Pairs, triads, small groups (4-6), larger groups (7+), whole group
Time	1-2 minutes, 2-5 minutes, 5-10 minutes, 10 minutes+
Resources	No resources, basic consumables (paper and pens), artefacts, objects and images
Space	No space required, a little space needed (table tops), lots of space required (training room floor area)

Table 2.2 Links for more icebreaker activities

Title of resource	Web link
Icebreakers, team-building activities, and energizers	http://tinyurl.com/gs2um7z
40 icebreakers for small groups	http://tinyurl.com/pubvpxv
Icebreakers and energisers	http://tinyurl.com/mjxjmlo
40 ice breakers and other warm-ups free from Training-Games.com	http://tinyurl.com/8a8tegl

Getting ready to learn

You are likely to be aware of other kinds of activities that you can incorporate into your training – these include mental warm ups, (re-)energisers, games and exercises. Some of these can be easily integrated into training plans and used at different times during a training session/day in response to participant or training needs:

- Re-energisers – use to maintain energy levels of participants first thing after coffee break/ lunch or when they are visibly 'starting to flag' (note their facial expressions and body language).
- Games (traditional and digital) – use to help participants either acquire educational content or apply taught input within an engaging and interactive learning context.

We have coined the umbrella term 'Getting Ready To Learn' (GRTL) to describe the different kinds of activities highlighted above; you are discouraged from referring to them as warm-ups as this is a term specifically associated with important physical education/sporting practices. What we mean by GRTL is that the activities you engage participants in are focussed on learning – this is where you either adapt the activity so that it has a clear learning focus or you are able to draw relevant learning from the activity as opposed to it simply being 'something fun to do'. An example of how this can be applied is shown in Table 2.3.

Table 2.3 How to take a generic icebreaker activity and give it a relevant learning focus

Activity *Would you rather...?* (Adapted from Knox, n.d.: 7)	Place a line of tape down the centre of the room. Ask the group to straddle the tape. Then ask them 'Would you rather...?' questions, e.g. '...visit the doctor or the dentist?', '...eat broccoli or carrots?' or '...watch TV or listen to music?'. To respond to the question participants have to jump either to the left or right of the tape as indicated by the trainer.
Adapted into a GRTL activity	Offer participants pertinent questions related to the training focus. So, during some training on magic tricks we might ask questions like, 'Would you rather... make the audience feel clever or 'stupid?' or '...do close-up' tricks or large-scale demonstrations?'
Learning to be drawn *from* the activity	Invite participants to discuss with the person in front or behind them what the different terms used in the question mean (revisiting previous learning), their reasoning for their response (justifying the application of new learning to a work context), or the difficulties that they had in making a choice and why (promoting critical thought).

This shift from thinking about the activity to the learning will help participants to see the point of GRTL activities ('NO TIME WASTERS, PLEASE!'), especially if you have a clear objective for using them, examples of which might be to:

- prepare the brain (and body) for learning;
- revisit and reinforce previous learning;
- build on previous learning;
- link previous learning to new learning;
- introduce new learning.

In summary:

- You are encouraged to get to know your participants at the start of the training session/s in an effort to build working relationships and offer participants personalised training.
- It is important to think carefully about the relevance of GRTL activities as participants should not see them as 'just a bit of fun' or as an unnecessary 'filler'.

Table 2.4 Recommended readings and resources

Source	Title	Author/s	Year	Web link
Journal article	Training and the needs of adult learners	Ota *et al.*	2006	http://tinyurl.com/y8h4u55
Project paper	Teaching adults: What every trainer needs to know about adult learning styles	Post	n.d.	http://tinyurl.com/7jrwc8l
Workbook	The Ultimate Educator: Achieving Maximum Adult Learning Through Training and Instruction	Edmunds *et al.*	2002	http://tinyurl.com/oxyyfks

Guess the link

| Starter | Individual | Some preparation needed | Multiple pictures related to your topic/focus | 10–15 minutes |

Project onto the screen two, three or four related images and ask people to tell you what links them (for example, a photograph of a dinosaur and the surface of the moon*). Ask participants to tell you the connection between the pictures. This can be an engaging way to help to start to share your learning aims for the session. If you can think of images to suit several different topics, then you can put different sets on each table and participants can go around and spot the connections (in groups or individually). This has the added advantage that the most quick-thinking individuals are less likely to spoil the fun for everybody by shouting out connection.

Benefits	This is a very quick activity, and it is non-threatening.
Considerations	If someone seems to get the connection straight away, then politely ask them to keep their rationale to themselves whilst asking others to add more detail.
Set-up tips	Clearly this works best if you have not yet told participants what the learning aims are for the training. This will only sometimes be appropriate.
	It is tricky to set this activity at the right level as the connections may be too easy or too obscure. It is better to go for too obscure than too easy as most participants will enjoy offering numerous guesses.

Ask the participants to think of other images that could link to those you have shown them.

 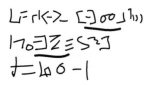

Invite participants to write down a sentence that connects all of the images together.

Instead of just having pictures that are all related, you can have an 'Odd-One-Out' round with three pictures that are connected with one that is not.

* Our link for this was asteroid impacts – wiping out the dinosaurs and creating impact craters on the moon.

Jumbled up picture

Display an image that links to your learning aims but that is obscured or hidden in some way, and ask participants to suggest how the image links to the focus of the training. You can cover up sections of the image which you reveal slowly, or you can use Photoshop, PowerPoint or another image editing package, and apply one of the artistic filters on a high setting (such as swirl, blur or mosaic) to obfuscate the image.

Alternative – Start a normal image very small and zoom in slowly asking participants to shout out when they can see the link (use the animation 'grow' in PowerPoint).

Wordplay

Try to spell out a word or phrase related to your learning aim using images (do an online search for 'Simon Drew puzzles' for many excellent examples). You do not have to do the drawings yourself; use clipart to make it easier/quicker to create.

GOOD GOOD BE BE TRUE

Alternative – If you are feeling particularly creative you can try to create a Dingbat that relates to your learning aims. These are words or phrases that are disguised or hidden by being jumbled up. Do an online search for 'Dingbats puzzle' for numerous examples.

Mime

Divide your participants up into small groups, and give each group one of your learning aims for the session. Each group has three minutes to come up with a mime for your learning aim, which the others will have to guess. You may have to give groups a maximum of twenty seconds to act out their mime, and then give other groups a minute or so to guess. This gives participants a chance to meet one another, but also helps them to clearly understand what the aims of the session are going to be.

Extension – If they cannot guess easily within a minute, the mimers are allowed to say one word as a clue.

Jigsaw

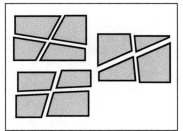

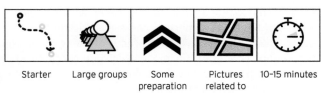

| Starter | Large groups | Some preparation needed | Pictures related to learning aims cut up | 10–15 minutes |

Prepare in advance pictures related to your topic or focus, a different one for each group, and cut up the pictures so that there is a 'jigsaw' piece for every member of the group. For example, if you need three groups of four, cut up three different pictures each into four pieces. When the participants arrive, give out the pieces at random and ask participants to find people to complete their picture. Once they have joined together in their groups, give them a question or task related to that picture, e.g. 'What is happening in this picture?' or 'What do you think caused this to happen?' This activity, and the others on this page, are ways of grouping your participants whilst also getting them thinking about the training topic.

Benefits ▪ You can quickly tell who is likely to be dominant within the groups, and can start assessing their baseline knowledge.

Considerations ▪ A picture that can be interpreted in a number of ways is likely to result in more interesting discussions.

Set-up tips ▪ If there is one section of the image that is more important than the rest, it may be worth cutting through it (so it is not completely obvious to any one participant).
▪ If you have pieces of any jigsaw left over, tell participants where they can find them to complete their jigsaw.

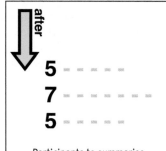

Participants to summarise their image for the rest of the group by creating a simple haiku (a Japanese poem made up of three lines consisting of five, seven then five syllables respectively).

Each group has to prepare a drawing of what happens next, which they present as feedback to the rest of the group.

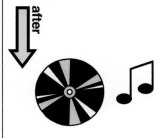

Participants have to decide what songs should form the soundtrack to this picture, which they then present to the rest of the group.

Confidence line

Ask participants to line up in order of their confidence about how they feel about one of your learning aims. Ask, for example, 'How confident would you be to explain topic X to someone else?' Now go along the line and number them 1, 2, 3, 4, 1, 2, 3, 4, 1, 2 ... (or however many groups you want) and ask them to group together by number. This is a non-threatening way of creating mixed ability groups –
you acknowledge that some people are not confident
yet and also that some people are very experienced
and comfortable with the topic. By explicitly setting
up these roles, the more experienced members may
enjoy the training more as they feel they are
supporting others (as well as learning themselves).

Thought-provoking thingies

Put a number of thought-provoking drawings, puzzles, tests, questions or other activities around the room and ask participants to circulate and choose the one that they would most like to explain to the rest of the group. Give a limit to the maximum number of people that can choose each task. As participants walk around the room
they will automatically end up thinking about all of the
examples you have set out, and they should start discussing
the 'answer' to their activity with the others in their group
before they have to feedback to the whole group.

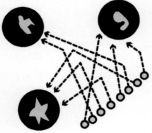

Alternative – Ask participants to give feedback on the task
they understand least well to encourage them to ask others
questions as they walk around the room.

Self-selection

One of the easiest ways to group your participants is to let them self-select. You can make the groups more balanced if you give participants advice about how they should select their groups, for example, 'Please try to make sure there is someone from every group who is confident about explaining X, Y or Z.' You may well do this half-way through a training session to vary the group dynamics, and you can ask participants to 'work in new groups of three, with people that you have not sat or worked with yet.' This is also
a good way of separating participants that know each other
well.

Alternative – If the group knows each other well,
ask one of the participants to do the grouping for
you.

Rules, OK?

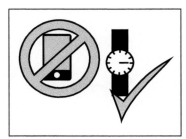

| Starter | Whole group | Very quick to prepare | Flipchart or computer | 10–15 minutes |

Ask participants to contribute to a list of 'group rules' that will help to ensure that the training sessions are efficient, participants are supportive of each other, and that distractions are minimised. As participants call out ideas for rules, check that each rule is clear to everyone and that they can all agree to it. If everyone is happy with the rule, write it up on a flipchart or type it onto a computer that is being projected (or ask a participant to record it). These rules can cover anything from punctuality, what participants should do if their mobile phone rings or if they receive a text, when to check emails, or how they should behave in group discussions.

Benefits
- This is most useful if you are going to be working regularly with the same group of participants over a number of days or weeks.
- We have both mentored trainers who have had groups that are regularly distracted by mobile phones and/or emails. Trainers who had generated group rules and then enforced them from day one were much less likely to have interruptions or participants who were disengaged.

Considerations
- Many training groups will not need this, and you may be happy to manage any issues as and when they arise.
- However, if you think it may be needed, it is easier to set this up at the start of your training rather than apply it retrospectively.

Set-up tips
- Writing the rules on a flipchart is quick to do and is useful because you can tear it off and display it on the wall. Typing the rules onto a computer works well if you would like to alter the wording or the order of the rules in response to later discussions.

If someone is still using their phone, and you want to avoid confrontation, mention to the whole group that you have spotted someone on their phone, and kindly ask them to please stop using it.

If this has still not worked, you can ask participants to monitor one another, and point out that it is distracting you (and potentially them) from the training (bit of peer pressure!).

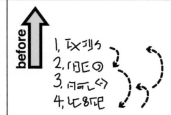

List some rules that you have pre-prepared and ask participants to put them in order of importance. This is a quicker activity, but can still positively influence participant behaviour.

Transform yourself

Ask participants to draw an annotated sketch of themselves in their current role and what they want to look like after the training (or after three months, but as a result of changes coming from the training). This simple idea can ensure that participants are reflecting on what they want to achieve from the training (looking forwards). It also helps them come up with realistic expectations for the training session and encourages them to take responsibility for ensuring that a transformation occurs. This is more suitable for courses lasting a day or longer. As participants are drawing, you will have time to go around and see what the common needs are.

Alternative - Ask participants to interview each other in pairs to work out how they will change as a result of the course.

Brick-to-brick, back-to-back

Split the group up into pairs and ask them to sit back to back. Give participant A in secret a small abstract *Lego™* model you have made, built from around 15 bricks (glue these together if you will use them regularly). Now give participant B the exact same bricks they will need to build the model. Without being able to see each other's model, A has to describe to B how to build it. You can make it harder by adding more bricks or easier by creating a recognisable shape. As well as being an excellent icebreaker, this activity is particularly suitable for developing clear communication skills between participants.

Extension - Try out the activity again but this time 'B' is not allowed to say anything!

Group Roles, OK?

Ask participants to form groups and assign different roles to members. If this does not happen naturally you can encourage it by assigning or rotating the roles. The roles you use will depend on the next activity, but it could be a **Leader** who keeps the groups organised and liaises with you, a **Recorder** who ensures everyone agrees and records any decisions, a **Sceptic** who asks the difficult questions and checks the whole problem has been discussed, and a **Summariser** who brings together all the points and provides feedback when needed.

Extension - Ask participants to decide what the role titles should be, as well as choosing who does what.

References

Dunlap, D. (2013). *Games and icebreakers for the ESL classroom.* Available at: www.fulbright.cz/sites/default/files/soubory/gamesicebreakers.pdf (accessed 22 November, 2015).

Edmunds, C., Lowe, K., Murray, M. and Seymour, A. (2002). *The Ultimate Educator: Achieving Maximum Adult Learning Through Training and Instruction.* Washington, DC: Office of Victims of Crime, US Department of Justice.

Knox, G. (n.d.). *40 icebreakers for small groups.* Available at: https://insight.typepad.co.uk/40_ice breakers_for_small_groups.pdf (accessed 8 December, 2015).

Ota, C., DiCarlo, C., Burts, D., Laird, R. and Gioe, C. (2006). Training and the needs of adult learners. *Journal of Extension,* 44(6) Article 6TOT5.

Post, H. (n.d.). *Teaching adults: What Every Trainer Needs To Know About Adult Learning Styles.* Bloomington, MN: Pacer.

Sisco, B. R. (1991). Setting the climate for effective teaching and learning. In: Hiemstra, R. (ed.) *Creating Environments for Effective Adult Learning.* New York: Jossey Bass Inc. (pp. 41-49).

The University of Manchester (n.d.). *Students as partners: Peer support icebreakers.* Available at: http://documents.manchester.ac.uk/display.aspx?DocID=7582 (accessed 22 November, 2015).

Snapshot B: Planning

Let's play a game of 'Spot the difference'. Which of the following questions should you ask yourself when starting to plan some training?

- What is it that participants should do?
- What is it that participants need to be able to do?

We strongly believe that your starting question should be: 'What is it that participants need to be able to do?', and so your first task should be to determine what the **learning aims** are for your session before starting to think about the **activities** that you will use in your training (Mann, 2004). This is the first stage of the *A-frame of training* (see Figure A, page 4).

If you are looking for a consistent and reliable method to plan your training, then we are afraid you will not find it here. There are many different approaches that we use, but they all begin with the key idea: **aims** before **activities**. Approaches include:

- **Planning with sticky notes** – On each sticky note is a brief description of an activity that you are going to use and underneath it, in smaller text, is written the learning aim(s). Move the sticky notes around until you are happy that the training order flows nicely and that all the learning aims are covered. You can even use different coloured sticky notes to help give you balance to your session: for example, green for participant-led activities and orange for trainer-led activities. This works particularly well when you are co-planning with someone else. Try the Post-it Plus app to record and save your final plan when you have finished.
- **Planning in columns** – Write the learning aims across a long piece of paper and then underneath each one start writing ideas about activities that could be used. Cross ideas out and scribble arrows all over the paper as you change your mind about the order of events.
- **Planning with the presentation** – Starting by planning with the presentation sometimes makes sense. To avoid the tendency to be too activity-driven, start by writing simple slides with the aims listed on them, and get the order of the aims correct before describing any activities. We find that starting with the presentation tends to work well for courses that are similar to other courses that we have led in the past. The 'Slide Sorter' view in PowerPoint, or 'Light Table' view in Keynote, where you can see all of the slides at once, gives you the best overview of your training day, and enables you to move them around easily.
- **Planning on the bike** – A lot of planning actually occurs before you put pen-to-paper or finger-to-keyboard, and this is done whilst walking or cycling around, or even in the shower! If you scribble down your thoughts on a piece of paper when you get back, then having this starting point will make planning a little less daunting.

Once you have planned the aims and activities for your session there are three documents that may be of help for you to create:

1. **Day plan** – This is a list of the activities that you will do on that session/day and the order in which you will do them. This can be handwritten or typed, but try to keep it to a single piece of paper, if possible in a large font: it is a guide to remind you what to do on the day when you will not have time to read lots of text.

2. **Kit list** – This is a list of the resources that will be needed on the day. If several different people are preparing the resources (for example, you are taking some and the venue will provide others), then split this kit list up by the person responsible for bringing each set of resources.
3. **Course overview** – If you have a session that covers multiple days, then it is helpful to create a course overview document detailing the learning aims you have for each of the sessions. This will be helpful for you to 'see the whole package' and for participants to understand how the sessions will link together.

Battle plans do not survive beyond first contact with the enemy.

Paraphrased from Helmuth von Moltke

Although it may not be helpful to think of participants as your enemy, we have offered you some sound advice above as there are clear parallels with training. Your 'battle' will not go well if you rigidly stick to your initial plan. We are not saying that having a plan is a bad idea (far from it!), but you should not be too prescriptive and you need be able to adapt and respond to the needs of your participants on the day. To that end, whilst it is helpful to estimate timings for activities, it is a good idea to plan in some flexibility; this can be achieved by adding some activities near the end of the training that can be 'squeezed' down if needed, or planning an extension task or two if the group are finding your other tasks too easy. You may also find it easier if you estimate the timings for a block of activities rather than trying to estimate the exact timings for each activity in isolation, e.g. 'These four activities will take me to break-time'. Do not forget though to also allow time for participants to reflect on their learning (Plymouth University, 2010).

The final piece of advice to help with planning is to give yourself feedback on each piece of training that you run. On your day plan you should indicate which parts have taken you longer or less time than expected, identifying any tasks that you did not get to do or were not success-ful, and any good questions the participants asked for which you had not been prepared. This will be a big help next time when you will not necessarily remember exactly how it went.

Table 2.5 Recommended readings and resources

Source	Title	Author/s	Year	Web link
Article	'Reflection' learning development	Plymouth University	2010	http://tinyurl.com/jgchztc
Book	Teaching in the Lifelong Learning Sector	Scales	2008	http://tinyurl.com/j9mkbtd

References

Mann, S. J. (2004). *Guidelines for writing aims and intended learning outcomes at the programme and course level.* Available at: www.gla.ac.uk/media/media_105307_en.pdf (accessed 1 November, 2016).
Plymouth University (2010). *'Reflection' learning development.* Available at: www.plymouth.ac.uk/uploads/production/document/path/1/1717/Reflection.pdf (accessed 1 November, 2016).
Scales, P. (2008). *Teaching in the Lifelong Learning Sector.* Maidenhead: Open University Press.

Chapter 3

Establishing existing knowledge

Alan says:

“ As part of my role I often help and support experienced teachers who are running training and support at other schools. From one of these observations is an example that stands out in my mind for all the wrong reasons, and highlights one of the differences between the delivery style needed for teachers of adults and teachers of children (see Snapshot L for more information).

The trainer stood up at the beginning of the session for a science department of 15 teachers and said, 'My name is Dr. Julius Narcissus, and I solved Fermat's Last Theorem.'* He then proceeded to tell an entire department about the achievements he had in his school and lectured the assembled teachers about what they needed to do overcome any problems.

Unfortunately, this overconfidence did not go down well with many of the delegates, most of whom were really good teachers and at least half had been teaching for longer than he had. They remained polite on the day but were angry when I received the evaluation responses afterwards. The inability of the trainer to recognise the participants' experience, and to build upon it, meant that most of the good ideas that he was sharing were lost.

This approach may have worked perfectly well for school-age pupils, or even for different groups of less-experienced adult learners such as initial teacher trainees, but we need to be aware of showing humility, particularly when running training for peers. **”**

When planning a training session, there seems to be so many things to think about:

- Where will the training be taking place?
- How many participants will be attending?
- What electrical equipment will I need to take with me on the day?
- When do I need to have my handouts prepared by so there is sufficient time for them to be photocopied?
- Who is sorting out the catering (if appropriate)?
- What am I actually going to be teaching participants during the training?!

It is important to carefully consider the final bullet point above because there are numerous trainers who just think about what they want to teach within the parameters of the session title. However, Jarvis (2004: 144) argues that 'adult learners bring years of previous knowledge and experience to the classroom, as well as an established system of values and beliefs that govern their thought'. You should be mindful of this because participants' existing knowledge can and should influence the content of the training delivered – there is no point 'going over old ground' if participants already know it! Whilst revisiting existing knowledge helps to consolidate and strengthen it in participants' minds, there is a danger that some trainers are likely to be greeted with participants wearing frustrated 'I-know-all-of-this' facial expressions when they are delivering. In this chapter introduction we will consider how this can be avoided by exploring the why, the when and the how trainers can establish the existing knowledge of participants, not only to support their training but, more importantly, their participants' learning.

*Both the name and outrageous achievement have been changed.

NOTE!
Let us be clear about what we mean by 'existing knowledge'. Whilst various typologies (classifications) of knowledge exist (see de Jong and Ferguson-Hessler, 1996), for the purposes of our discussion we are referring to:

(a) declarative knowledge (the knowledge of facts and concepts), and

(b) procedural knowledge (knowing how and when to apply various procedures, methods, theories, styles or approaches) (Carnegie Mellon University, n.d.).

Please also note that the words 'existing' and 'prior' are used interchangeably in the remainder of this chapter introduction.

The *why*

We have already touched on why establishing existing knowledge of learners is important for trainers and participants. Naturally, there is more to it than just that! Take a look at the summary statements which have been adapted from Zull (2002) below:

1   In order to effectively communicate with participants, trainers need to find a common language; this can be based on prior knowledge.
2   Prior knowledge is always the beginning of new knowledge; new knowledge builds on existing knowledge.
3   Prior knowledge is persistent and is not easily swept away simply because a trainer says something else is true.

These summary statements emphasise the key role that existing knowledge has on new learning: they are dependent on each other! Carnegie Mellon University (2015) supports this, arguing that participants' existing knowledge can 'influence how they attend, interpret and organize in-coming information. How they process and integrate new information will, in turn, affect how they remember, think, apply, and create new knowledge.' Indeed, trainers who make it clear that they are assessing the participants' prior knowledge and then strive to build on this are less likely to come across as patronising, and so will gain participants' trust. It is therefore important that trainers establish the existing knowledge of those who attend their training. So when and how can this be achieved? Let's deal with the when first!

The *when*

Virtually all trainers would say that the best time to establish the existing knowledge of participants is before the training actually takes place. It makes sense, especially if you have time to reflect on participants' collective responses; with this information you can positively 'shape' the training to build on participants' strengths whilst targeting misconceptions or address areas for consideration (we prefer this to the rather negative-sounding 'weaknesses'). However, some participants may be unwilling or unable to share this information with trainers in time, and so it may be necessary to establish existing knowledge during the training, building in opportunities throughout the session for participants to 'activate' (bring to the forefront of their minds) what they already know/think they know. The training input that is delivered thus responds to this existing knowledge as it is established in the session. This is based upon good Assessment for Learning (AfL) practices where you are responding to the needs of the participants as opposed to simply following a script or training plan to the letter (see Chapter 11, Assessment).

Interestingly, existing knowledge can also be established after the training session when participants are invited to reflect on their learning from the training: 'How did your prior knowledge help you to increase your understanding of the new knowledge that you have been introduced to?' 'Looking back' helps participants to make connections, not only between their existing and new knowledge, but also between 'the theory' and how this relates to/impacts on 'practice' in the workplace (Schön, 1983). Let us now consider the how!

The *how*

There are various strategies that you can choose from to establish the existing knowledge of participants. We considered some of these in Table 3.1, but we also need to consider the ways in which this information can be gathered. Most trainers use various forms of technology to ascertain the prior knowledge of their participants, e.g. sending out emails with attachments, texting hyperlinks to online questionnaires, or talking to participants virtually via Skype or FaceTime. Some participants prefer the good old 'pen-and-paper' approach that sees trainers seeking information using posted documentation. We have listed some creative tasks that you can set your participants in Table 3.1 to engage them before your training. Other ideas are explained in more detail in the remainder of the chapter.

Once this prior knowledge has been successfully gathered it is then crucial that trainers actively do something with it! Quality suggestions, partly based on the thinking of Ambrose *et al.* (2010), include:

- Look carefully for patterns of strength and error in participants' responses.
- Tweak or adapt your planned taught input, practical activities and printed materials in light of this new knowledge.
- Make participants as a whole group verbally aware of their knowledge that is collectively both secure and in need of development during the training.
- Emphasise how the session is positively responding to their prior knowledge during the session to reinforce its value (see, it was worth doing!) and highlight the quality of the training they are experiencing.

In summary:

- Good training calls on trainers to take note of participants' prior knowledge, either before and/or during the delivery of the training.
- Participants' prior knowledge, if accurate and sufficiently activated, can provide a strong foundation for building new knowledge.
- The more connections that are created with participants' relevant prior knowledge during the training, the greater the depth and/or breadth of their new/future understanding.

Table 3.1 An overview of strategies that may be used to establish existing participant knowledge

Strategy	Brief explanation
Fact or fiction	Offer participants a series of different statements which they have to identify as either being true [fact] or false [fiction].
3-2-1	Get participants to write a list of three things that they already know about the training focus, two things they would like to learn more about, and one question related to the key concept or learning core (adapted from Lewis and Thompson, 2010).
Survey	Present participants with a variety of question types – for ideas, see pages 8-12 of http://tinyurl.com/h67ucgr – that help to gather the prior knowledge of participants in relation to the main course content.
Visualise it!	Suggest that participants bring with them a drawing/concept map/sketch/diagram/3D model/picture/photograph that summarises their prior knowledge of the core content of the upcoming training.
Continuum	Present participants with a number of statements to which they need to make a 'scaled response', e.g. on a scale of 1-5, 1 being *Not clear at all* and 5 being *Absolutely clear*.
Video	Using their smart phones, invite participants to record and send you a five-minute face-to-camera video of them talking about what they know linked to the training focus.
What's wrong?	Offer participants a detailed summary of the training session. Include in it some deliberate mistakes (factual, **not** spelling, grammar or punctuation-related) for participants to identify and comment on.
Wordle	Get participants to create a Wordle (a word cloud) that is specific to the upcoming training. See http://tinyurl.com/jdbn4mn for some interesting alternatives.
KWL grid	A true classic! See Chapter 8 Doing for information about this strategy. An alternative is the LINK grid (attributed to Alston) where participants complete the first two columns (L and I) prior to the start of the training:

L	I	N	K
(**L**ist everything you know)	(**I**nquire about what you would like to know)	(now make **N**otes)	(what do you **K**now now?)

The remaining two columns are completed during the training session (column N) and at the end of it (column K).

Table 3.2 Recommended readings and resources

Source	Title	Author/s	Year	Web link
Article	Learning in interactive environments: Prior knowledge and new experience	Roschelle	1995	http://tinyurl.com/j8csxtj
Book chapter	Beginning with what students know: The role of prior knowledge in learning	Campbell and Campbell	2008	http://tinyurl.com/y7jk54sc (and then click on the Preview tab)
Essay	What they don't know can hurt them: The role of prior knowledge in learning	Svinicki	1993-1994	http://tinyurl.com/gwptmj4

Question-board

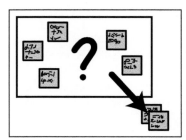

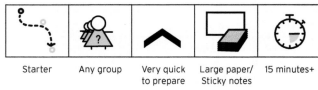

| Starter | Any group | Very quick to prepare | Large paper/ Sticky notes | 15 minutes+ |

Use this when introducing a topic that participants already know a bit about. Give everybody an A3 (or bigger) sheet of paper with a large question mark written in the middle. Ask participants to write down on sticky notes any questions related to the topic that they then attach to their sheet, either individually or as a group. As you are talking, or as a group discussion is going on, the participants can remove any questions that are answered. At the end of the task each participant or group will have a small selection of questions left over, giving a personalised list of items that they do not understand. These can then be addressed individually or as a group.

Benefits
- This promotes independent reflection of understanding.
- The question-board improves participants' concentration whilst you are doing some direct teaching/input.

Considerations
- With some groups you may want to display the stems 'Who? What? Where? Why? How? When?' to help improve the questioning.

Set-up tips
- Your room setup will be important (see Snapshot A, Learning Spaces). Initially you just need to ensure that everybody can see and hear you clearly, but if you want interaction later on you may want to set up the room like a conference hall so that everybody can clearly hear and see everyone else.

| Participants write down one of their unanswered questions and then go away and research the answer, bringing back an answer to share with the group. | Everybody stands up who has got a question left, and only sits down once their question has been answered. | In a group of up to eight, participants create a poster using the different sticky note questions and write on the poster the answers to recap/ embed the learning. |

Stickyhead

All of the participants write a question that they have about a topic on a sticky note; these can then be lightly stuck to their head. They then walk around the room asking others to answer their question. You can then ask the participants that have had their question answered to a satisfactory level to sit down so you only have to answer the remaining questions that have not been answered.

Alternative - You can ask participants not to answer the questions but rather group them together with similar questions so that you can see what the main concerns or unknowns are.

Difficulty islands

Using string, create three areas of the floor to represent the **Easy**, **Medium** and **Hard Islands**. Participants are to think of some questions about a topic that they have already studied, writing their name and questions on individual sticky notes, which they then put on the relevant islands. Other participants have to choose a question which they then answer for the original author, who tells them if they have answered it satisfactorily.

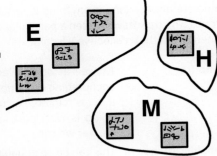

Extension - To turn this activity into a competition, each participant can start with five tokens (in the form of sweets, stars, etc.); whenever they answer someone's question satisfactorily they have to give them a token. The person with the most tokens wins.

Precognition planning

It can be powerful to know beforehand what questions need to be addressed and answered. Sometimes you can ask for these to be emailed to you so that you can collate them to inform your session; sometimes you will have to ask for them at the start of the session. Early on in your training ask participants to put the questions in the order that they would like them to be answered (hence prioritising them).

Alternative - Rather than asking them to be emailed in, you can give participants access to an online forum so that they can see each other's questions to avoid repetition. Other participants may well answer some of the questions on the forum before the session even begins.

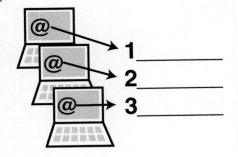

Special delivery service

| Main | Individually | Lots of preparation needed | Cardboard post-boxes, questions, postcards | 25 minutes |

Distribute around the room a few post-boxes or large envelopes, each with a pre-written question stuck to the front of them. The participants are to go around the room and write answers on postcards, which they then post into the appropriate post-box. Then, split up the participants into enough groups so there is a small group for each post-box. They have to read the answers that have been offered and decide which is the most complete answer (and if anything is missing). Participants are then to explain to the other groups why they have chosen a particular answer so that everyone (including the trainer) can benefit from their collective wisdom.

Benefits
- As well as acknowledging the most appropriate answer, you are also encouraging reflection about the answers provided.
- It helps reinforce a culture where it is acceptable to be wrong; all we are doing is working together to iteratively improve and reach the best answer we can.

Considerations
- This can be an engaging way to ascertain knowledge, especially if you, as the trainer, do not need to know exactly who has contributed each answer.
- If the questions require short answers then it is reasonable to ask participants to answer all of them; if the questions are more open-ended it may be more appropriate that participants only answer one or two each.

Set-up tips
- A cereal box with a rectangular hole cut out makes the perfect, easy-to-build post-box. However, they can look more attractive if you turn them inside out and re-glue them.

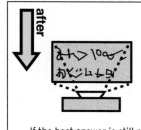

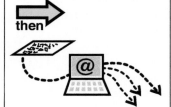

| If the best answer is still not complete, share it (possibly using a web-cam/visualiser and projector) to seek more ideas/responses from participants. | Once a complete answer has been agreed, ask one participant for each question to type up the answer and send it around to all of the other participants. | Compare the participants' answers with your answer or a 'textbook' answer, and ask participants to identify and comment on the similarities/ differences. |

Flip on this

When you ask for a list of items it can be very helpful to write down the answers offered by the participants, e.g. after asking a question 'List the factors affecting...'. You can write them down on a flipchart or type them directly into a word processor, if you have a projector attached. This can be really informative for a trainer to see what is missing, or misunderstood, so that the training can focus on these areas. It is often helpful to write down everything almost verbatim; if you change the wording too much you may end up assuming the participants have the same knowledge as you, whereas it may need to be addressed separately.

Post-it Placard*

When the topic you are looking at has a selection of connected facts you can ask participants to write each piece of knowledge on a sticky note, joining them together to create a hand-held placard. They can then take the placard around to share and compare ideas with others, and can add to it as required.

Alternative – This also works particularly well for helping to structure debates, or when comparing different approaches, for example if there are conflicting ideas or theories.

Comprehension questions

Ask participants to consider a topic and then stimulate a range of answers by asking them to consider it using a range of simple questions stems that you have pre-emptively displayed around the room: Who...? Why...? Where...? How...? When...? Which...? This can promote a wider range of answers than if you give participants no stimulus, as they will start to consider the problem from different angles. The open interpretation of a question like 'Who?' can often be interpreted in a range of different ways for the same topic: Who invented it? Who does it affect? Who implements it? Who benefits? Who loses out?

Alternative – You can use much more specific questions if you have very clear learning aims that your participants need to achieve.

*Other sticky notes are available (but they are not alliterative with 'placard'!).

References

Ambrose, S., Bridges, M., Lovett, M., DiPietro, M. and Norman, M. (2010). *How Learning Works: 7 Research-based Principles for Smart Teaching.* San Francisco, CA: Jossey-Bass.

Campbell, L. and Campbell, B. (2008). *Mindful Learning: 101 Proven Strategies for Student and Teacher Success.* Thousand Oaks, CA: Corwin.

Carnegie Mellon University (n.d.). *The educational value of course-level learning objectives/outcomes.* Available at: www.cmu.edu/teaching/resources/Teaching/CourseDesign/Objectives/CourseLearningObjectivesValue.pdf (accessed 22 July, 2016).

Carnegie Mellon University (2015). *Assessing prior knowledge.* Available at: www.cmu.edu/teaching/designteach/teach/priorknowledge.html (accessed 21 July, 2016).

de Jong, T. and Ferguson-Hessler, M. G. M. (1996). Types and qualities of knowledge. *Educational Psychologist,* 31(2), 105–113.

Jarvis. P. (2004). *Adult Education and Lifelong Learning: Theory and Practice,* 3rd edn. London: Falmer Press.

Lewis, A. and Thompson, A. (2010). *Quick Summarizing Strategies to Use in the Classroom.* Available at: www.gcasd.org/Downloads/Summarizing_Strategies.pdf (accessed 7 September, 2017).

Roschelle, J. (1995). Learning in interactive environments: Prior knowledge and new experience. In: Falk, J. H. and Dierking, L. D. (eds) *Public Institutions for Personal Learning: Establishing a Research Agenda* (pp. 37-51). Washington, DC: American Association of Museums.

Schön, D. (1983). *The Reflective Practitioner.* New York: Basic Books.

Svinicki, M. (1994). What they don't know can hurt them: The role of prior knowledge in learning. *Essays on Teaching Excellence,* 5(4). Available at: http://podnetwork.org/content/uploads/V5-N4-Svinicki.pdf (accessed 16 May, 2016).

Zull, J. E. (2002). *The Art of Changing the Brain: Enriching Teaching by Exploring the Biology of Learning.* Virginia: Stylus Publishing, LLC.

Snapshot C: Preparing resources

The resources that you need to deliver some training will vary significantly depending on the topic you are teaching, and whether you have access to your own regular training venue or have to move around between different training venues (you are an itinerant trainer). As having different training venues is likely to be challenging, this is what we will focus on in this practical Snapshot.

Let us delve into Alan's laptop rucksack-of-many-pockets! He takes it to all his training courses. In it we find the following:

- his laptop and charger
- a phone and charger
- a computer/projector adapter (to connect HDMI from his computer into VGA for some projectors)
- a wireless presenter remote
- a small wireless mouse
- a connector to join his phone to the projector, so that if necessary he can share photos he takes on the day
- several sets of sticky notes of various sizes and colours
- a set of six chunky whiteboard pens of different colours
- a set of around 20 poster pens: some chunky, most not
- a handful of normal pens/highlighters
- a couple of blank USB pen drives
- a few paper clips, a bit of Blu-tack, a pencil sharpener and a ruler
- a calculator
- a set of mini-whiteboards and pens (not every day, but most days)
- a full water bottle
- some paracetamol tablets
- a nice teabag.

Once he knows what he is taking, Alan asks the person responsible for the training venue to provide the following:

- a parking space
- a projector with screen and cables
- an electrical socket for his laptop
- a Wi-Fi code for him (and possibly the participants)
- a flip-chart (or a whiteboard, etc.)
- fruit and drinks on arrival, snacks and drinks at break and a good lunch.

This seems to be a good regular minimum for Alan. But of course he also packs and/or requests the learning/assessment aids he needs and any session-specific equipment required. When carrying resources to a venue he has found that a combination of stacking boxes with lids and fabric bags for books/papers is the easiest to handle. Simon, on the other hand, prefers to use his trusty fold-away plastic trolley!

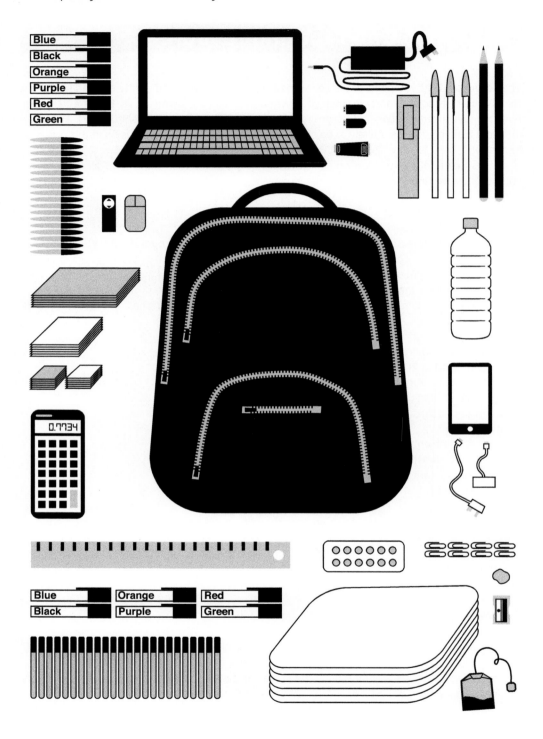

FIGURE 3.1 The bare necessities

On arrival at the venue, Alan's first priority is his stomach and he checks the food has been sufficiently prepared, but his next priority is that he can get his computer working with the projector and to get onto the network if needed. The computer may well not be the most important part of the day, but it is the item that can take the longest to fix if a specialist is needed.

Paper resources

There is a definite compromise to be made when deciding what photocopying to take with you. As well as the environmental considerations of photocopying too much, there is also the chance that participants may be overwhelmed with information: if there are only two articles that are key to your training, then participants are more likely to read and value them if they are the only two handouts they take back to their professional setting. See Snapshot G, Handouts for practical advice on how to effectively prepare handouts.

For most courses, a transparent plastic wallet offers an attractive, cheap and compact way for participants to collate their resources together. You can buy these wallets with a card slot on the front so that they can be professionally branded, and giving them your card means that participants can get in touch with you again easily post-course.

If you are not responsible for arranging your own photocopying, then a useful way of arranging your copying is to put all of the documents in subfolders, clearly labelled with how many you need, whether they are needed in colour, and if a non-standard size is required. For example, for the copying on Alan's last course with 20 participants he had the following subfolders:

- 2 black and white A3 copies
- 2 colour copies
- 5 colour copies
- 10 colour copies
- black and white copies per participant
- colour copies per participant

He asked for two copies of some materials that were extension tasks, five copies of materials that were for group work, ten copies of some worksheets to be completed in pairs, and then copies for each participant of a diagnostic test and his course notes.

Electronic resources

If you know your venue will support easy internet access for all of your participants, then it is possible to share your resources electronically. There are several formal ways of doing this, such as Cisco WebEx, Adobe Connect, Microsoft Lync Server and Google Docs. However, it may be easier to share them through a simple cloud-based repository, such as Google Drive, Dropbox, Microsoft OneDrive, etc. Please consider that participants may like to make notes during the session and that the act of writing (rather than typing) is likely to help them to remember (see Boch and Piolat, 2005).

Because Alan delivers training at a wide range of venues, he does not trust the Wi-Fi to work well enough to be the only method of sharing materials, so he relies on paper copies on the day of the course. At the end of a course, Alan shares all of the resources he has used with participants using a cloud-based repository.

Table 3.3 Recommended readings and resources

Source	Title	Author/s	Year	Web link
Booklet	Evaluation and selection of learning resources: A guide	PEI Department of Education	2008	http://tinyurl.com/hfnse9h
Website	How to publish documents online: 8 great ways to share documents with others	Lifehacker	2014	http://tinyurl.com/jgokecz

Reference

Boch F. and Piolat, A. (2005). Note taking and learning: A summary of research. *The WAC Journal*, 16, 101–113.

Learning phase 2

Direct input of new ideas

Chapter 4

Sharing new knowledge (with presentations)

> **Alan says:**
>
> " There are a few times when I have been observing a training session by an experienced teacher, which has then turned into a 45–60-minute lecture with an entirely passive audience of teachers or trainers. I certainly have my doubts about the efficacy of this approach (and the feedback usually matches this summary), but I also believe this is particularly bad for a room full of teachers. No matter what the topic being covered during that session, the trainer has missed an opportunity to model successful, active teaching, and there is an increasing danger that the teachers are then likely to go back to their classrooms and lecture their students. "

A couple of questions:

1   How many of you have attended training where the trainer used a PowerPoint presentation to share new knowledge with you?

     We suspect virtually all of you.

2   How many of you have attended training where the trainer used a PowerPoint presentation that can only be described as 'awful'?

     We suspect many of you!

Microsoft PowerPoint is a staple component of what most people encounter as part of their training experience. As a tool, PowerPoint is a valuable resource for trainers given how relatively easy it is to use. However, there are numerous criticisms of PowerPoint, with Tufte arguing that PowerPoint leads to 'an over-reliance on a hierarchy of ideas, over-simplification, and linear thinking on [the] part of the presenter and audience' (cited in Brock and Joglekar, 2011: 86). This chapter introduction initially considers five of the most common mistakes that trainers make when using PowerPoint to share new knowledge with participants, identifies why these occur, and suggests practical ways that these mistakes can be effectively addressed (Table 4.1). Before we continue, however, we would like to draw your attention to two key points:

1   We recognise that there are alternative presentation creating tools that trainers can and should use to aid their training, e.g. Prezi, Keynote, PreZentit, Google Slides, FlowVella, Sway, Powtown, Haiku Deck, emaze, SlideDog and Sozi. However, we will refer to PowerPoint in this chapter introduction, given that it is by far the most popular presenting software.

2   Presentations of any type should not just be talking (remember that we have participants, not listenants); there is a whole lot more that we can use as part of our presentation to increase interactivity and engagement, and ultimately improve the learning of participants. Ways that this can be achieved include using:

     ▪ short quizzes or game play, e.g. 'Real or No Real' [True or False] (credited to DJ Scott Mills, Radio 1)
     ▪ Think-Pair-Share talking opportunities
     ▪ videos and 'live' demonstrations
     ▪ participant polling with raised hands or the showing of coloured cards
     ▪ scenarios for participants to problem solve
     ▪ short writing activities, e.g. the three-minute summary or creating a glossary of new key concepts.

Further ideas can be found in the remainder of this chapter.

Table 4.1 Techniques to improve your presentations

Mistake 1: Too much text!

Explanation:	This is the most common mistake trainers make when creating a PowerPoint presentation. Each slide that is shown is filled with dense text that is too small to read, is presented in a 'sea of bullet points', or contains spelling, grammar and punctuation errors.
Reasoning:	This typically happens with novice trainers – they want to give participants **everything** so try to cram it all onto the slides. This also occurs when trainers are insecure in aspects of the subject knowledge they are to train others about.

Practical ways to address this:

- Only present the most important information.
- Use only three to four bullet points on each slide. Remember to use bullet points if they help to highlight key areas or make the presentation simpler for participants to follow.
- Ensure that the text you use on the main part of the slide is sized at least 20.
- Try to limit the number of words you present on the slide (35-40).
- Use subtle text-effects to draw participants' eyes to key ideas that are presented in a clear font, e.g. Arial.
- Replace text with a picture if it 'says' what you want it say!

Mistake 2: Way too many slides!

Explanation:	Just think how disheartening it is for participants to find out they are going to have to endure 84 PowerPoint slides and that all of these will be used before lunch! Having too many slides is frequently referred to as 'Death By PowerPoint'.
Reasoning:	This occurs because trainers think that they will be able to maintain participant interest by offering them tonnes of information. The problem is that after about the 25th slide, participants actually begin to lose interest!

Practical ways to address this:

- 10 to 15 slides are usually enough for a presentation of around an hour.
- Be selective! Once you have finished preparing your PowerPoint, go back and ask yourself: do participants really need this slide or not?
- Seek the support of a colleague to help you cut your presentation down, slide wise.
- Offer additional slides on a separate presentation which you can offer to participants (electronic/paper-based) as 'further reading'.
- Avoid putting a counter at the bottom of the presentation that states which slide you are on, for example slide 9/84.

Mistake 3: Colour catastrophe!

Explanation:	Imagine that you have created a PowerPoint to help participants learn about colour mixing so you decide to use colourful background designs and coloured text to 'jazz up' your presentation. However, you find that participants are distracted by the explosion of colour and have difficulty in reading the text on the screen/paper slides.
Reasoning:	Trainers understandably try to demonstrate their creativity by 'playing about' with standard aspects of the presentation template. Doing this, however, can cause unnecessary confusion and headaches!

Table 4.1 Continued

Mistake 3: Continued

Practical ways to address this:

- Keep it simple – use a plain white background as this creates a clean, professional look. Maintain a consistency to this throughout the entire presentation.
- If you want to colour the text, use high-contrast colours (dark on light).
- Avoid colour clashes – yellow does not 'sit well' on green!
- Think about those participants who are colour-blind – consider adopting a light blue background and avoid red text.

Mistake 4: Animation anarchy!

Explanation:	Imagine information in your presentation that 'appears' on different slides through zips, whizzes, zooms, rolls and swivels, much to the delight of … well … just you (the trainer).
Reasoning:	Again, in an effort to be creative, many trainers use animation to bring in, emphasise and remove information on different slides. However, for participants, this can make the presentation 'too busy' and it actually distracts them from the content of the slide.

Practical ways to address this:

- Remember that that content is more important than the 'flashiness' of the presentation. Use animations sparingly.
- Use animation to enhance the presentation, not divert from it, e.g. revealing an answer to a question you have given.
- Select just one animation scheme and apply it to all slides.
- The same idea (above) should also apply for slide transitions.

Mistake 5: Picture im-perfect!

Explanation:	Pictures, images, diagrams, drawings, sketches, graphs, tables – anything that is 'visual' on the slide is actually **not** discernible (or seemingly of value) due to its presentation, formatting, quality and positioning.
Reasoning:	PowerPoint is known as a visual presentation tool and so many trainers try to complement the text they offer with something graphic. However, distorted images, blurry photographs and irrelevant clipart items (that are poorly animated) unfortunately can irritate, confuse and spoil the presentation for participants.

Practical ways to address this:

- Only use strong, high-quality and bold graphics (2D not 3D).
- Offer only one or two 'visuals' per slide.
- Avoid images that have no meaning to the slide content/the presentation as a whole.
- If possible, choose an image against a plain background.
- Spend time thinking about the best position for the graphics to make each slide aesthetically pleasing.

The mistakes in Table 4.1 have principally focussed on the preparation of a PowerPoint presentation. However, good trainers acknowledge this is only the first part in the successful sharing of new knowledge with participants; the second part focusses on how the presentation is actually used by trainers. Whilst we have had to unfortunately endure some dire PowerPoint presentations in our time, we have also had to suffer some dreadful presentations of these presentations! By this we are referring to the delivery of the presentation given by individuals.

There is little worse than having a trainer simply read the content of each slide to participants – **this is simply unacceptable practice!** Other practices trainers may do that can be off-putting include:

- standing in front of the data projector screen
- talking at the screen
- talking down at their notes
- presenting in a quiet/monotone voice
- nervously *umm*-ing, *err*-ing and *like*-ing their way through the presentation
- talking too quickly
- standing too still or being constantly 'on the move', e.g. arms, legs, facial expressions
- rushing the last few minutes of the presentation to 'get it over and done with'.

Many of the behaviours above are simply a result of fear – the anxiety of presenting to others. However, as a trainer, public speaking is very much your 'bread and butter'! To overcome the above we advocate that you embrace the following:

- **Breathe deeply** before and during your delivery to control your emotions and maintain confidence levels.
- **Think** in a positive way to take your thoughts away from the negatives.
- **Rehearse** what you are going to say to others – does it make sense to them?
- **Visit the training room** beforehand to feel comfortable in the venue.
- **Practice eye-to-eye contact** with people as you present.
- **Be mindful** of your body positioning and movements.
- **Talk from your heart** and not from your notes.
- **Be excited** about what you are presenting by varying the pitch of your voice so that your audience is eager to hear about it.

'Instead of worrying about your delivery, find ways of improving it' (Carnegie, 2008: 10). You can do this by asking thoughtful questions, giving participants challenges, getting them to spot mistakes, helping them to make connections, and giving them time to reflect on what they see/read on the slides (remember to pause if you need participants to read something on a slide word for word). A nice idea is to seek ideas and suggestions from others, e.g. your participants!

In summary:

- There are many presentation tools available to support your training. We should use them to help our participants learn, but not through lecturing.
- Creating a PowerPoint is only the first part in its effective delivery; it is **how** it is delivered to participants that is of critical importance.
- There are simple ways in which you can overcome the anxiety that we all experience when presenting to an audience.

Table 4.2 Recommended readings and resources

Source	Title	Author/s	Year	Web link
Research review	What is the impact of PowerPoint lectures on learning? A brief review of research	Cornwell	2014	http://tinyurl.com/gwxxu3q
Handout	Creating an effective PowerPoint presentation	Schwartz	n.d.	http://tinyurl.com/h6gcgnh
PDF	Teaching with PowerPoint	Northern Illinois University	n.d.	http://tinyurl.com/yd48lds8

Conceptual questioning

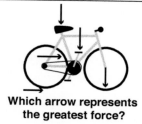

Which arrow represents the greatest force?

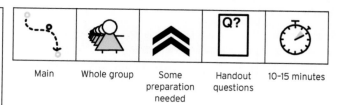

| Main | Whole group | Some preparation needed | Handout questions | 10–15 minutes |

Display a multiple-choice conceptual question. This question should not be testing recall, but should focus on the ability of participants to think and understand a topic using their existing knowledge. Give participants a minute to think about it by themselves. This gives you a chance to reflect and plan your thinking for the next part of the session. Mazur (1997) calls these types of questions ConcepTests, and lists the stages to get the maximum interaction from his audience (which was university undergraduates):

1 Question posed (1 minute).
2 Participants given time to think (1 minute).
3 Participants convince their neighbours (peer instruction; 1–2 minutes).
4 Feedback to teacher: tally of answers (1 minute).
5 Explanation of correct answer (2+ minutes).

You can optionally ask participants to record their answers before and after their discussions, but often this is not needed.

Benefits   ▪ By encouraging the participant to make a decision they have to think much more deeply about a problem rather than simply being told the answer.

Considerations   ▪ The formulation of the questions is paramount and may take you a while to get the level right; you may also find that some questions you think are good do not work as well as expected. Questions should focus on a single concept, have adequate multiple-choice answers, be unambiguously worded, and not be too easy or too difficult (Mazur, 1997).
▪ It is helpful to think about the concepts you wish to teach before you have written the rest of the presentation.

Set-up tips   ▪ Display the questions on a PowerPoint for speed of use, or give out handouts if you want participants to recall these ideas later.

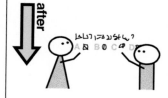

Participants have to try to convince their close peers that they have chosen the correct answer, whilst explaining their reasoning. You can listen in on their answers and ask questions to develop thinking.

Participants feedback their answers to you (either by a show of hands or by an electronic method such as *Socrative.com*).

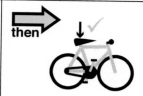

You explain the correct answer to the whole group, responding to the answers that were given.

CLOZE

A Cloze question is one where some words have been removed, and participants are given a choice of words they can use to fill in these blanks. You can remove the words at random (every seventh word, for example), but you will usually have more interesting conversations if you remove the keywords. There are several websites that can help you to create these easily, for example http://mrmartineau.github.io/cloze-test/

> taxi   man   paths
>   roads   boy
>
> **How many ___ must a ___ walk down, before you call him a ___?**

Make it harder - Add challenge to this activity by giving multiple similar words that can be used to fill in a blank. You may be happy if some participants have identified any of the 'correct' words, but the strongest participants can then debate which is the 'most correct'.

Spot the mistake

Display a picture or a piece of text and ask the participants to spot the mistake or anachronism. Many people love a challenge like this, and there is often someone who will be prepared to argue vociferously if there is any ambiguity in your text. However, this is a good opportunity for these participants to have a say in a controlled manner where you have clearly given everyone permission to be pedantic and pernickety.

Alternative - You can have a series of mistakes and participants have to count the mistakes.

Count the daisies

If you have a lot of slides in your presentation and you want an easy way to ensure that participant attention is maintained, you can ask them to count something that appears occasionally throughout your presentation. This can be something linked to your topic; for example, 'Count the new keywords I have introduced – they are underlined', or 'Count the number of times I have written Florence Nightingale's name'.

Alternative - The real reason for doing this may be to keep the attention on your presentation, so you can simply ask participants to keep an eye on the number of flowers/Smurfs/cakes etc. pictured throughout your presentation.

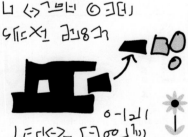

Asking quick questions

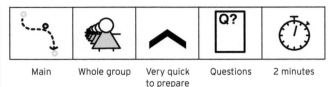

Main　　Whole group　　Very quick　　Questions　　2 minutes
　　　　　　　　　　　　to prepare

Do not forget to break up a long presentation by asking a quick question to your audience. A question can be a 'closed' question – usually one that is factual and requires a short answer. However, you can usually generate more conversation and discussion by asking an 'open' question – these questions do not usually have definitive answers and are often asking for lists, definitions, explanations of how something works, or an opinion. Depending on the situation you may wish participants to call out the answer, put their hands up or write down the answer. If you have access to a set of mini-whiteboards then you can ask questions that need a short written answer, but also questions that need a picture or diagram to answer.

Benefits
- The biggest advantages of asking an occasional question is that once participants know they may be asked some questions they will be encouraged to listen.
- You can use quick questioning to find out if your learning aims have been met or if you need to go back and recap something.

Considerations
- A strong way of planning your training is to start by deciding what questions you are going to ask. This helps to ensure that training sessions meet their learning aims, because the presentation will be linked around the participants' ability to answer these questions.

Set-up tips
- To remind you to ask questions periodically, add them as slides to your presentation. You can even add a blank slide or a question mark so that it is just a reminder to you.
- Try to give participants at least five seconds of thinking time before you take an answer from them (count 'One elephant, Two elephant, etc.' in your head).

At the start of a session ask a question that participants cannot answer yet, but do not give the answer straightaway. At the end of the session ask your question again.

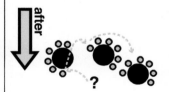

If you have been given a good answer but one that is not complete, keep asking other participants to give you more information until you have a full answer.

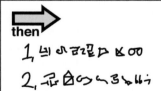

At the end of your presentation display all of the questions that were asked, inviting participants to write down answers to the two questions they have found most challenging.

Handout reflection time

One of the most common ways of ensuring that participants are engaged is to give them handouts of your presentation so that they can make notes as you go along. Some participants will make good use of these straight away, whilst others will do so only if you remind them. Ensure that after every 'chunk' of your presentation participants are given a couple of minutes to reflect on what has been covered and write down some notes. If you are using PowerPoint or a similar application you can choose to print only the key slides by printing a 'Custom range' of slides, and 'Handouts' (3 slides per page). Whilst this takes more forethought it can be very helpful to focus the participants on your main aims, plus it saves some trees.

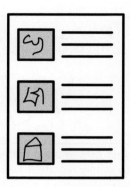

Video interlude

A good way to break up a presentation can be to play a video clip. To get the most out of a video you need to be aware of why you are going to use that video: what are your learning aims, and how is the video going to help you achieve these? You may well end up deciding that only a short section of the video is needed – sometimes as little as twenty seconds – and very rarely as long as ten minutes. Often you can get more value from the time spent watching a video if there is a task that participants have to complete whilst watching the

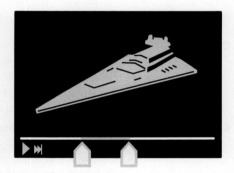

video, for example, 'Answer these three questions'. YouTube has a helpful feature to skip the unwanted sections at the start of their videos: you simply right-click the video and then select 'Copy video URL at current time'.

Tracking progress

Another way of improving interaction and encouraging full participant attention is to give them a set of questions which they have to answer during the presentation. These questions are more effective if they are short/closed in nature, and it is a good idea to give participants a couple of minutes before your presentation so that they can read and 'digest' these questions otherwise participants may miss something you are saying whilst they are reading/answering your questions.

   Alternative – You can also give participants a list of your learning aims which they are to tick off when it has been satisfactorily covered.

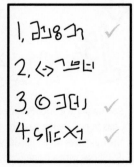

Draw the reading

| Starter | Pairs | Some effort to prepare | A piece of writing/ plain paper | 25 minutes |

Sometimes you may have a small, very important section of your presentation that you want to ensure that all participants listen to but you do not want to simply restate it five times. This activity is an excellent way of ensuring that participants are listening but it requires that you write down in advance exactly what you are going to say. As you are reading, ask your participants to draw themselves a series of pictures to act as memory-aids. Tell them that they will be asked to recollect their learning afterwards from their sketches. You then need to follow the next two steps (linked below) to ensure that it has been memorised/learned by the participants.

Benefits
- This can be a really effective way of improving engagement. When we have tried it with a section of text containing 35 facts, nearly all participants recollected 30+ by the end, with most retaining 33 or more.
- It is a nice way of differentiating a session because often participants who excel at this may not appear the most confident or the most able.

Considerations
- You will have to pause frequently whilst talking to allow participants to catch up or keep up.
- If someone is struggling you can boost their confidence by saying, 'It's usually the person that finds it hardest that does the best.'

Set-up tips
- You may want to encourage participants to write numbers and a letter or two, but disallow complete words.

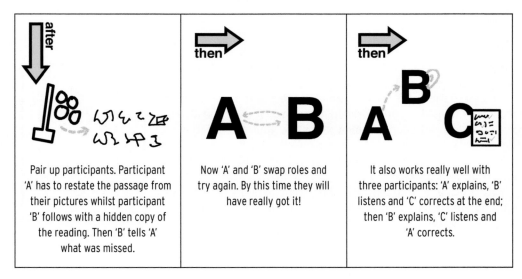

after

Pair up participants. Participant 'A' has to restate the passage from their pictures whilst participant 'B' follows with a hidden copy of the reading. Then 'B' tells 'A' what was missed.

then

Now 'A' and 'B' swap roles and try again. By this time they will have really got it!

then

It also works really well with three participants: 'A' explains, 'B' listens and 'C' corrects at the end; then 'B' explains, 'C' listens and 'A' corrects.

Tell me back

If you have a section of your presentation that is particularly important you can invite one of the participants to come up and re-teach it again to the whole group. This will enable you to check that individual's understanding but will also highlight the importance of this section to the other participants by giving them two 'listens'. If you have a confident group who have all been paying attention you can pick anyone at random after you have finished speaking. However, there are often times when you will want to select someone in advance and 'prep' them so they know they will have to re-teach it when you have finished.

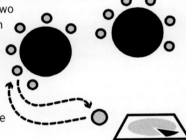

Alternative – Motivate everybody by saying 'Someone will be invited to re-teach this at the end.'

Countdown conundrum

Embed a simple game as a single slide during your presentation to enliven the atmosphere without going off-topic. Examples include:

- Countdown conundrums – Display an anagram of one of your keywords that they have to unscramble.

- Hangman – The classic game for children that can be played using one of your keywords.

- The Million Pound Drop Live – Give four answers to a question and ask participants to decide how much of a million pounds they would be prepared to gamble on each answer.

- Only Connect – Can participants spot the connection between a selection of phrases (first show them two phrases, then three, then four)?

- Just a Minute – Ask participants to explain a topic for sixty seconds without hesitation, repetition or deviation (they may use the topic phrase repeatedly).

Music with slides

If there is a section of the presentation where several slides have writing which 'says it all', then maybe you do not need to say anything during these slides. Most presentation software enables you to add some music that will automatically play and get the slides to automatically 'roll over' to the next slide. If you play with this you can easily create a series of slides that will explain what needs to be understood without participants having to listen to you. This shift of presentation style can re-ignite people's interest and shifts the emphasis for understanding onto them rather than you 'presenting'.

Alternative – A series of connected images can be very thought-provoking with music playing at the same time.

References

Brock, S. and Joglekar, Y. (2011). Empowering PowerPoint: Slides and teaching effectiveness. *Interdisciplinary Journal of Information, Knowledge, and Management*, 6, 85–94. Available at: http://ijikm.org/Volume6/IJIKMv6p085-094Brock545.pdf (accessed 21 August, 2016).

Carnegie, D. (2008). *Speak more effectively. Part one: public speaking – a quick and easy way.* Available at: www.dalecarnegie.com/assets/1/7/SpeakingEffectively.pdf (accessed 21 August, 2016).

Cornwell, L. (2014). *What is the impact of PowerPoint lectures on learning? A brief review of research.* Unpublished. Available at: www.hagerstowncc.edu/sites/default/files/documents/14-fletcher-power point-research-review.pdf (accessed 17 May, 2017).

Mazur, E. (1997). *Peer Instruction: A User's Manual (Series in Educational Innovation).* Upper Saddle River, NJ: Prentice Hall.

Schwartz, Michelle (n.d.). *Creating an effective PowerPoint presentation.* Toronto: Ryerson University. Available at: www.ryerson.ca/content/dam/lt/resources/handouts/EffectivelyPresentingContent.pdf (accessed 17 May, 2017).

Snapshot D: Teaching chains

If you sit down for a relaxing evening, which would you prefer to watch: a film or a selection of ten-minute unrelated 'shorts'? Assuming, like us, you would prefer to watch the film, then the question is why? Each of them can help to 'pass the time', each of them will tell a story, and they can provide you with the opportunity to smile, think, laugh or even cry. But the film is likely to be easier to watch and will probably be more engaging than a selection of unrelated shorts. So, why does a film hold our attention? It is because it builds throughout, at times telling different stories but ultimately weaving them into 'a whole' with a consistent message. This is how your training should feel.

When putting this book together, we were conscious to avoid just collecting together a group of activities that trainers can pick and choose from. The training you deliver should actually resemble a film. A variety of activities is great; different participants will engage more actively with some of your activities than others, but ultimately this mix of activities has to come together to tell a coherent story. To give training a consistent flow, we should try to ensure that the activities we use are thematically linked and allow for progression – we call this combination of ideas a **teaching chain**. Learning can therefore become 'a trajectory of development that connects knowledge, concepts and skills within a domain' (Heritage, 2008).

Let us look at a simple example of a teaching chain, used with trainee primary teachers, building on their existing knowledge about space and the universe:

Task 1

Arrange for groups of six trainees (add or remove questions for different sized groups). We start by asking a range of simple questions:

- What is the sun an example of?
- What are there eight of that orbit the sun?
- Which iced interlopers have an elliptical orbit around the sun?
- What do we call a collection of billions of stars?
- What is the name of the rocks that orbit between Mars and Jupiter?
- What is the name for all of the galaxies, and everything?*

As someone from each group shouts out the answer, one person from each group writes the answer in large letters on an A4 piece of paper until all six people have a different answer on their paper.

Task 2

Now we offer a range of harder tasks. Each group of six trainees works together with each trainee responding on behalf of the item they are holding. For example:

- Hold the paper above your head if you give off your own light.
- Hold the paper above your head if you are in the solar system.

*Note: The answers to the questions are star, planet, comet, galaxy, asteroid and universe

- Hold the paper above your head if you are on a circular orbit.
- Stand in order of size.
- Stand in order of closeness to London.

The fact that some of the tasks above have ambiguous solutions is great. The ambiguity will encourage discussion, which is ultimately what we want in our training.

Task 3

We now ask our trainees to place their words randomly on the floor and then to use them as stepping stones to generate a sentence that links the word they are stepping from and to. Encourage the most confident trainees to link the more difficult words together.

Task 4

Finally, we ask our trainees to go back to their desks and write definitions for each of the six terms, concentrating in particular on adding any new information they have gleaned through the different activities.

In the teaching chain example above you should see that at each step along the way we have been using the same key ideas and the same materials but that the level of difficulty, or independence in working, has increased with the latter tasks. Another thing to note is that the example above is deliberately designed to be non-patronising: the trainer does not have to give any help until it is needed, and if all of the trainees are confident and knowledgeable then the activity is extremely quick and the trainer can move on to other things.

Where possible, throughout this professional book, we have tried to encourage teaching chains by suggesting further activities that can be used before or after some of the main activities; however, we encourage trainers to develop their own teaching chains. Many of the best trainers who we have undertaken formal observations of have run sessions that flow smoothly and show progression: they have created teaching chains, even if they do not know our name for it. To encourage everyone to work towards this same gold-standard of training that flows, we provide a short summary:

- To make your training a smoother experience, try to develop teaching chains that are thematically linked.
- Teaching chains should show progression, either by increasing the level of difficulty or by increasing the participants' independence.
- Try, where possible, to make the transition from one activity to the next as smooth as possible by reusing materials.

Table 4.3 Recommended readings and resources

Source	Title	Author/s	Year	Web link
Research	Providing challenge and engagement in classroom learning for G&T students*	Williams	2012	http://tinyurl.com/zgksdcg

*Note: Suggestions made in Williams (2012) can be easily adapted for the adult training context, and activities for adults should also 'include higher order thinking skills, have perceived utility and also a meaningful outcome'.

References

Heritage, M. (2008). *Learning progressions: Supporting instruction and formative assessment.* Available at: www.k12.wa.us/assessment/ClassroomAssessmentIntegration/pubdocs/FASTLearningProgressions.pdf (accessed 1 November, 2016).

Williams, C. (2012). *Providing challenge and engagement in classroom learning for G&T students.* The National Academy for Gifted and Talented Youth. Available at: http://tinyurl.com/zgksdcg (accessed 18 May, 2017).

Chapter 5

Sharing new knowledge (without presentations)

Simon says:

> **❝** There are times when I just get bored of using PowerPoint. It becomes a formulaic expectation of participants when they come to training sessions, so I feel it is important that as a trainer I 'shake things up' a little! I remember a colleague once saying that they delivered a 1.5 hour session just using pictures and images and I was both amazed and shocked that this was indeed possible! It takes great confidence to move away from the security that a presentation offers trainers (it is a bit like a lesson plan that everyone can see), but when you have strong subject knowledge and are clear about what you want to communicate to others then it is just a matter of choosing a suitable mode and giving it a go! I have built up quite a trainer's toolkit of resources that I can use to support the training I deliver – the best resources allow participants to visualise either the ideas being advocated or the impact of these for learners. For example, I have developed an effective model called the Ice-Cream Cone Model (ICCM) to help teacher researchers 'build' small-scale action research questions – when participants see the question components being formulated and re-arranged to construct the full question, they can appreciate how easy and effective it is to use. Having a large ICCM template to hand reminds me that seeing is believing! **❞**

We opened the previous chapter with a couple of questions, the first of which asked how many readers had attended training where the trainer used a PowerPoint presentation to share new knowledge. We suspect that virtually every reader will have responded with a resounding 'Yes'! However, let's ask the question again in a slightly different way:

1   How many of you have attended training where the trainer did **not** use a presentation, like PowerPoint, to share new knowledge with you?

We suspect some of you.

2   How memorable was the presentation-absent training?

Probably quite memorable!

But what made this training memorable? Was it highly interactive? Did it really make you think? Was it a humorous experience? Did you have success when trying out some of the new ideas back in your place of work? It might be argued that it had something to do with the novelty of being trained without a presentation; indeed, with reference to PowerPoint, Tratt (2014) argues that '[e]veryone's used it, everyone's heard of it, and a lot of people are pretty tired of it'. This brings us to the first in a small series of FACTS which are associated with the chapter focus of sharing new knowledge without presentations:

FACT 1: It is possible to share new knowledge with participants without using a presentation.

For those of you who are new to the 'training game' this is a big risk, particularly as visual presentations typically offer trainers a 'safety net' to fall back on if they should 'dry up' (Davis, 1997); it is a bit like teacher trainees having a detailed lesson plan they can refer to if they forget the next part of their lesson. We would never advocate you trying to deliver training that you have not prepared; what is argued is that you do not need to have a presentation to accompany every training session that you deliver. Good trainers are likely to question how this is possible. The remainder of this chapter introduction seeks to offer some practical ideas to show how this can be achieved.

Steve Jobs famously said that 'People who know what they're talking about don't need PowerPoint' (cited in Issacson, 2011). This brings us to our second FACT:

> **FACT 2: You can share new knowledge with participants without using a presentation if you 'know your stuff'.**

Nickols claims that 'the ability to make powerful, polished and persuasive presentations derives from knowledge' (2003: 6). Clearly having strong subject knowledge is 'a must' if you are going to be considered a good trainer. It is said that you understand your subject if you can help others to understand it. Lloyd-Hughes (2016) suggests that good trainers both learn and share 'metaphors, poems … a famous example, a joke, quotes, powerful facts, collections of three or buzz phrases to repeat' with participants to aid subject knowledge acquisition. Other ways that subject knowledge can be shared and learned include writing up key terms or sketching diagrams up on a flipchart/whiteboard, conducting a real-life demonstration or distributing printed cards that summarise 'the key facts'. For these strategies to actually work, trainers need to offer an accompanying oral presentation that **introduces**, **informs**, **explains** and **clarifies** the subject knowledge. But how can this be done effectively? We can answer this with our third FACT:

> **FACT 3: Good training requires that you are able to verbally share new knowledge with participants both clearly and concisely.**

The FAO (1998) states that '[m]en and women in training positions are expected to be highly competent at presenting ideas, giving directions and explaining procedures'. In light of this, the oral skills of trainers need to be strong so that they can get their message across with speed and efficiency. To verbally share new knowledge with participants effectively means that you should think about:

- your voice (in terms of its tone, pace of delivery, pronunciation and use of expression)
- your word choices (be they simple, complex, technical or colloquial)
- your ability to articulate yourself with real understanding.

Huggett (2013) suggests that trainers can improve their voice delivery quality by listening back to recordings of themselves; we recommend that you also seek constructive criticism from your peers, family and friends when you practice in front of them, and participants who actually attend your training (both during and at the end of the session).

It is worth remembering that it is not just how something is said but what is actually said. This brings us to our fourth FACT:

FACT 4: New knowledge is best shared when it is linked to real-life experience.

Cross (1999: 5) is adamant that 'learning is about making connections'. As a trainer it is your role to help participants to make and understand these connections. Connections can be made between different ideas/subjects/theories/readings/research findings/discussions – anything that supports participants in 'seeing the links' that are directly related with the training focus. One important connection relates to the lived experience. Ideally these should be based on your own professional practice (recent or current), but they can also be drawn from the experiences of others that you know or have read about, or they can be invented to highlight your point. Post validates our assertion, suggesting that 'successful adult learning must relate to a lifetime of experiences' (n.d.: 5). You are also encouraged to help participants to make connections to their own experiences, seeing how the new knowledge you share with them supports, challenges or extends aspects of their professional role.

Whilst this chapter introduction (and its subsequent activities) considers ways in which trainers can share new knowledge without presentations, this is not to say that you cannot use other visual aids to assist you. We have given mention to several aids on pages 72-78 but there are, of course, many others that can be utilised with care, consideration and a little creativity! This leads us beautifully to FACT 5:

FACT 5: New knowledge can be shared with visual aids that are not presentations.

It is said that a picture says a thousand words. We argue that the same can apply to models, drawings, videos, objects, displays, handouts, brochures, posters, artefacts and exemplars.

From our experiences of training others, we know that participants respond well to the use of visual aids, particularly as they help to break up the rhythm (monotony?) of listening, and direct their attention to something that is not … us! We particularly like giving participants time to actually 'handle' the aids, discussing them with their peers and reflecting on them as part of group discussions – this quickly stimulates interest and activity that, in turn, promotes valuable learning. businessballs.com (2016) takes this practice further, advocating that visual aids can be used 'for various themes and metaphors', including the following examples:

- 'toolbox with tools – toolkit (set of products, tools, methods, materials, documents, etc., each designed for a specific purpose, and related to the other tools in the kit).' [theme]
- 'paper plane – aim high, explore, strive.' [metaphor]

Good trainers recognise that training sessions should not be saturated with an abundance of visual aids – e.g. charts, grids and diagrams – but aids should be used sparingly to support the sharing of new knowledge. By doing this it helps participants to retain more of the knowledge they encounter by providing them with a concrete example for conceptual thinking, and (hopefully) makes their learning a bit more 'permanent' (adapted from Shabiralyani *et al.* 2015: 226).

In summary (the five FACTS):

- It is possible to share new knowledge with participants without using a presentation.
- You can share new knowledge with participants without using a presentation if you 'know your stuff'.
- Good training requires that you to be able to verbally share new knowledge with participants both clearly and concisely.
- New knowledge is best shared when it is linked to real-life experience.
- New knowledge can be shared with visual aids that are not presentations.

Table 5.1 Recommended readings and resources

Source	Title	Author/s	Year	Web link
Videos	How to Do A Presentation [Colin James Method]	James	2015	http://tinyurl.com/y9cyf34j
Short paper	Oral presentation skills: A practical guide	Storz *et al.*	2002	http://tinyurl.com/pnsgxyr
Web page	How to present well without slides	Berkun	2013	http://tinyurl.com/gvgenrc

Picture perfect

Main	Any group size	Some effort to prepare	Pictures in various formats, e.g. large posters, digital	5–10 minutes

As has been highlighted in the introduction to this chapter, it is said that a picture can say a thousand words – so why not display a stimulus picture for participants to discuss the significance of it to your training?! Share new knowledge by using visual aids in the form of pictures, paintings, drawings, sketches, illustrations or images. Other suggestions include comic strips, flow charts, logos, maps and diagrams. Using pictures allows you to talk around the image, verbally 'unpacking' it by offering participants clear explanations, responding to their questions, or having joint discussions. For those participants who learn from what they see, we have found pictures to offer wonderful variety to what they are typically offered in their training: a text-heavy PowerPoint presentation and the trainer!

Benefits
- A picture can stimulate participants' interest, particularly when they 'see' its relevance in supporting their acquisition of new knowledge.

Considerations
- Your choice of picture is crucial – participants need to clearly recognise its value in helping them to learn new knowledge. Google Images is a great starting source.
- Often images can clarify or enhance participants' ability to remember hierarchies and links between the ideas you need to discuss. An example of this is a pyramid built of several layers, with the most important layer on the top (but needing to be supported by the important layers below).

Set-up tips
- Try to use good-quality pictures at a high enough resolution.
- Think about the size of the picture you are offering participants – remember that it needs to be seen clearly by those at the back of the training space.

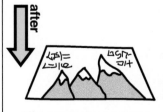

Offer participants an A4-sized copy of the picture you are using that they can annotate with their own personal notes.

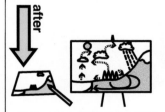

Encourage participants to sketch their own version of the picture you are showing them as an active way of reinforcing their learning of new knowledge.

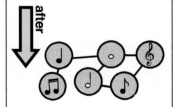

Suggest that participants create a picture of their own, combining your picture with their existing knowledge.

Click click!

Show participants appropriate photographs that you have taken on your smart phone or digital camera. Explain how 'the scene' visually represents a process, a thought, a skill or an attitude that relates to the new knowledge you wish to share with participants.

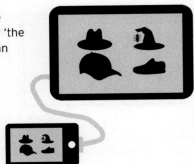

Alternative - Invite participants to take their own photographs throughout your training, or as part of the plenary, to visually represent the new knowledge/skills they have learned from you and their peers.

Complete the comic

Try drawing a simple comic strip but leave the final frame blank. Ask participants to come up and draw or make suggestions for what the ending could be. You can use this to highlight the correct way of doing something, or alternatively, the wrong way! This comic strip can include words or just be images.

Alternative - If the training focus is on developing a process or a way of dealing with something/someone, then show them a comic strip with the middle frame being in need of completion.

Graphic representation

With participants, share visual models of theories that underpin the new knowledge that you wish them to know. Sometimes you can find online interactive versions of some of these models to stimulate participant interest.

Alternative - Invite participants to work together to create 3D versions of the visual models they are introduced to, adapting these in response to their own creative ideas.

Surfaces for sharing new knowledge

| Main | Any group size | Some effort to prepare | Whiteboards, easels, large paper, pens | 5-10 minutes |

There are many 'alternative' surfaces you can utilise to share new knowledge with participants. The flipchart board, for example, is a great resource as it allows you to 'build' knowledge in front of your participants' eyes by making a visual record of keywords, bullet point ideas and small diagrams; this can be done by you or a willing participant ('your glamorous assistant'!). Mini-whiteboards are a versatile resource that can be used as large cue cards to introduce facts and figures, or they can be used as jigsaw pieces that can be put together to create a diagram that represents a theory in pictorial form. Other valuable surfaces include the walls or tables (with large bits of paper stuck to them) or windows (writing on them with whiteboard pens).

Benefits
- Presenting on different surfaces is an effective way of grabbing the attention of your participants ('Oh, now that's different!').
- Sharing new knowledge via these different surfaces helps you to capitalise on the learning potential that your training space truly offers.
- Key ideas can be left up on display, so that you can frequently refer back to them.

Considerations
- Avoid wasting valuable training time by physically writing everything down. Invite individuals to act as a scribe for you or prepare key information on pieces of card that can be easily displayed.

Set-up tips
- Ensure that you know what all of your key points are as you will not necessarily have any PowerPoint slides to help you remember!
- Practise your ability to talk as you write to maximise training time.

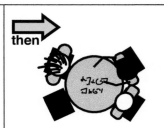

| Suggest that participants make their own record of the knowledge you share with them, as you share it with them either in written or visual form, e.g. taking photos on their smart phone. | Invite participants to share their understanding of your input with reference to the information on the surface you have been training at to revisit/strengthen their learning and understanding. | Encourage participants to 'model the model' by using different surfaces, e.g. the floor, a corridor wall or a small coffee table, to train others during your training session. |

The power of speech

Your most valuable resource as a trainer is your voice. The very best training is not down to zippy presentations or engaging activities but relates to your ability to articulate yourself in a clear, confident and expressive way. Build time into your training session where you simply talk with participants (not at them!), varying your projection, pace of delivery, tone and emphasis to stimulate participants' learning through what they hear.

Alternative – Video record yourself 'talking-to-camera' during which you share with viewers a new piece of knowledge. Play this as part of your training session as an interesting method of knowledge sharing.

Perfect props!

Capture participants' imaginations by putting together a 'prop box' that contains objects, artefacts and resources that you use as a reference point when sharing new knowledge. Ensure that these have relevance to your training focus, getting participants to guess the significance of certain items as part of your input.

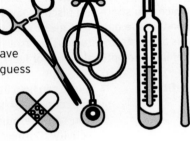

Alternative – Create a simple feely box which participants can use to feel, describe and reveal props which you refer to as part of your training input.

Are you sitting comfortably?

Share new knowledge with participants by telling them a story that is based on real events or your imagination. Tailor the story to your audience in relation to the five elements of story: **characters** (educators), **setting** (learning environment), **plot** (application of a theory, strategy or idea), **conflict** (a difficulty or issue the educator has in applying the theory, strategy or idea), and **resolution** (how it all turns out okay in the end).

Alternative – Provide participants with real or imaginary written case studies that exemplify your learning aims applied to a practical context.

Musical mayhem

| Main | Any group size | Some preparation needed | Music – various formats, e.g. downloads, CDs | 5–10 minutes |

Music can be used as a powerful way of helping participants to learn and remember new information and experiences during your training sessions. Research suggests that playing certain types of classical music can engage both sides of the brain for more efficient learning, reduce errors in adults' understanding, improve creativity and clarity, and maximise learning time (see http://tinyurl.com/ybxu4bkj). By playing music in the background, you can create a comfortable learning situation in which you share and discuss new knowledge with your participants – this does, however, depend on the genres of music that you choose to play! Positive mood music, movie soundtracks and instrumental music can all impact on the way that participants feel. This helps them to get into the optimal mood for learning, and can be memorable.

Benefits
- Music can help to reduce participants' stress levels, which can negatively impact on their capacity to learn during your training.
- You can use music as an indication to subtly change the focus of an activity: 'During the music please continue to work, but review your progress and check that you have enough time left to complete today's task.'

Considerations
- Remember to play music at an appropriate volume.

Set-up tips
- Ensure that you know how to work the music player with speed and efficiency so that valuable learning time is not wasted in dealing with operating issues.
- Invest in an extension cable so that any musical equipment you need is 'close to hand' despite the location of the power supply.

As you play music in the background, accompany this with some participant body percussion ('You make the music!') to help rote learning of some new knowledge.

Turn the music volume down, offering participants some musical silence for them to reflect on their rote learning.

Get pairs of participants to verbally take it in turns to share their rote learning with each other as music plays in the background – when the music stops their turn ends!

Putting words to the music

Share with participants simple chants, mnemonics, raps, jingles, rhymes and song lyrics that help to teach/reinforce new knowledge as part of your training. Model these and encourage participants to join in and perform them with you, as appropriate.

Alternative - Invite participants to add their own words to well-known tunes (from their childhood or popular culture) based on new information or knowledge they have been introduced to. Simple songs such as nursery rhymes can work more easily.

Music videos

Show participants appropriate videos from YouTube which use the creative arts (music, dance, drama, song) to present new knowledge to them as training participants. These could also serve as a valuable learning resource to share with their learners back at their place of work.

Alternative - Suggest that participants collaborate together to create their own mini music video to promote 'peer teaching' and share new knowledge that they have acquired with other participants.

'What's your jam?'

As a pre-course task, ask participants to create a playlist of their favourite pieces of music, bringing this to the training with them on a portable listening device (MP3 player, smart phone). Suggest that they listen to it as they engage in independent activities (e.g. desk research) as part of your training in an effort to create a connection to the information and provide a trigger for recall.

Alternative - Invite participants to play their favourite track to the group as they discuss their personal learning from the independent activity they have engaged with. Can listening participants identify a connection (be it explicit or subtle) between the music and the new knowledge?

References

businessballs.com (2016). *Visual aids.* Available at: www.businessballs.com/visualaids.htm (accessed 23 August, 2016).

Cross, K. P. (1999). *Learning is about making connections.* The Cross Papers, No. 3. League for Innovation in the Community College.

Davis, M. (1997). Adult learning: The place of experience. In: Knight, P. T. (ed.) *Masterclass: Learning. Teaching and Curriculum in Taught Master's Degrees* (pp. 28–38). London: Cassell.

Food and Agriculture Organization of the United Nations (FAO) (1998). *Food quality and safety systems: A training manual on food hygiene and the hazard analysis and critical control point (HACCP) system.* Section 1 – Principles and methods of training. Available at: www.fao.org/docrep/W8088E/w8088e03.htm# (accessed 23 August, 2016).

Huggett, C. (2013). *The Virtual Trainer's Guide to Content Delivery: 5 Techniques To Deliver An Effective Virtual Class.* GoToTraining. Available at: www.cindyhuggett.com/wp-content/uploads/2016/08/5-TECHNIQUES-to-DELIVER.pdf (accessed 29 June 2017).

Issacson, W. (2011). *Steve Jobs.* London: Little, Brown.

Lloyd-Hughes, S. (2016). *Make your message stick: the 'RULE' of memorable presentations.* Ginger Public Speaking. Available at: www.gingerpublicspeaking.com/make-your-message-stick-the-rule-of-memorable-presentations/?utm_referrer=www.google.co.uk/ (accessed 23 August, 2016).

Nickols, F. (2003). *Effective presentations.* Available at: www.nickols.us/presentations.pdf (accessed 23 August, 2016).

Post, H. W. (n.d.). *Teaching adults: What every trainer needs to know about adult learning styles.* Available at: www.fastfamilysupport.org/fasttraining/Other/teachingadults-whattrainersneedtoknow.pdf (accessed 23 August, 2016).

Shabiralyani, G., Hasan, K. S., Hamad, N. and Iqbal, N. (2015). Impact of visual aids in enhancing the learning process case. *Journal of Education and Practice*, 6(19), 226–233. Available at: http://files.eric.ed.gov/fulltext/EJ1079541.pdf (accessed 23 August, 2016).

Storz, C. *et al.* (2002). *Oral presentation skills: A practical guide.* Evry: Institut national de Télécommunications.

Tratt, A. (2014). *5 fresh PowerPoint alternatives.* Haiku Deck. Available at: https://blog.haikudeck.com/powerpoint-alternatives/ (accessed 23 August, 2016).

Snapshot E: Technologies

There are two golden rules we consider important when considering **when** and **how** to use technology in your training:

1 **Technology should support and enhance your training** – Whilst it can be used to add variety and interest, avoid using technology just for the sake of it. If there are alternatives that will achieve the same aims just as effectively or efficiently, then you should probably use those instead.
2 **Technology can be temperamental** – There are many things that we can do to plan for problems, but unless you are training directly about the technology, it may be worth giving some thought to a back-up plan if the technology does not work.

However, when it is used well, technology will change the pace of your training sessions, give excellent opportunities for formative assessment (see Chapter 11, Assessment), and promote independent study. It is important to note that the technology you have access to will depend on whether you move from one training venue to another on a daily basis (an itinerant worker) or you have a fixed room that you will train in for many days, weeks, months or even years at a time.

Presentation

Let us assume that you want to provide some form of presentation using PowerPoint, Keynote, or something similar. It seems that almost everyone has had that awkward feeling when sitting at some training where the computer/mouse/projector/etc. has refused to work, and a present-ation has come to a grinding, painful halt. There are several practical ways by which we can reduce the chance of this happening, but these require some advanced planning.

Our main tip is to try to use your own laptop to present from where possible. In most sit-uations this is our preferred method for setting up our presentations. You will know how your laptop works and its quirks, you will know that your presenter remote ('clicker') works with it, all the software that you need is installed, and if someone asks a question that is off-topic you have access to all of your files with only a few clicks. The biggest challenge will be making sure that it can connect to the internet if you are in a new venue.

If you are not permitted to use your own device, or it is not convenient, then you will have to use the computer provided. Getting your clicker working may not be as simple as plugging it in, and you may need to check that all the file types you have can be opened on the machine – problem file types often include video clips, Flash files or Java applets. To get your files onto the computer you have two choices:

1 Use a cloud-based repository system (think Dropbox, Google Drive, iCloud) where all of your files are stored on the internet. This will require the laptop you are using to have a decent internet connection to download from. It does not often happen, but some computers have over-zealous filtering on their internet access.
2 Use a USB drive with all of your files pre-loaded. Again, you need to be careful as some com-puters are configured not to allow access to or from USB sticks for fear of computer viruses.

As an itinerant trainer, Alan makes good use of the ideas above. He will use his own laptop by preference, but all of his files are mastered on Dropbox, and so are accessible from any internet-enabled computer. As a final backup, he takes a blank USB stick with him, and if it is the only option, then he can copy the files from his laptop using that.

Top presentation technology tips

- Most projectors come with a remote that you can use to freeze or blank the screen. This can be really useful to freeze or blank the screen when you are setting up the next task, or if you want to check the upcoming slides.
- In PowerPoint or Keynote, if you need to pause your presentation to show a black screen then press the letter B. To pause your presentation and show a white screen, press W. To jump to any slide, just start typing the slide number and press enter. Press '/' in either application to see the other shortcuts available (support.office.com, 2016).
- If you are using your own laptop, make sure you disable your email/messaging client from giving you pop-ups every time you receive a message. Participants will find it very distracting, and may find out more about you than you would necessarily like. Also remember not to leave **that** holiday photo somewhere on the desktop screen!

Visualiser

One of the very best ways of sharing participant work, and demonstrating the process of giving feedback on a written task, is through the use of a visualiser. This is essentially a camera for showing objects/documents that can be easily connected to your projector. Used properly, 'visualisers can be used intuitively within a lesson, so they naturally complement existing teaching practice' (Becta, 2007).

Dedicated visualisers can be cumbersome and expensive, but you probably have most of what you need on your smartphone, i.e. a high-quality camera. To transform this into a portable, good-quality visualizer, you need to invest in the following:

- A phone/HDMI connector or a phone/VGA connector to connect your phone to the projector.
- A clamp stand with a flexible neck to hold your phone in position.
- A small light with a flexible neck in case the lighting is poor in the room.

All of the above can often be purchased for less than £10 each (unless you have an Apple phone, for which the adapter may be much more expensive). Having the ability to share participants' work, and to invite peer feedback, can usually be well worth the time and expense; consider it a valuable investment in enhancing the quality of your training!

'Bring Your Own Device'

For most training courses it will be reasonable to assume that most participants will have a smartphone with them, and they will know how to log on to a Wi-Fi network. This gives us the fantastic opportunity to get interaction from all participants in a variety of ways, e.g. for feedback, for formative and summative assessment (see Chapter 11, Assessment), and for independent learning. If you need participants to do more than a little reading online though, then you could ask them in advance to bring a laptop/tablet to your training. This is often referred to as Bring Your Own Device (BYOD), and is 'a variant of one-to-one computing whose time has come' (CDW, 2012). Being well prepared can make a huge difference to the quality of the experience for participants.

When planning your training you need to consider what participants will need to be able to access from their own device. Although most websites are now optimised for viewing from mobile devices, some older websites will not work as well, especially if they include Flash or Java applets.

If you have your own venue and you are setting up a guest Wi-Fi network, there are many choices to configure this. Even if you are not responsible for configuring the Wi-Fi network, it is worth knowing what your options are, especially when discussing it with the person responsible for setting it up. Some trainers may feel they do not have a choice, but they need to be aware that some Wi-Fi configurations will be easy for participants to use, others will not be as easy, and a sensible compromise will have to be made between security and ease of use. Options include:

- Guest Wi-Fi, with no password. **Easiest to use**.
- Guest Wi-Fi, with a password.
- Guest Wi-Fi, with no password, and a log-on screen that needs a code for that day.
- Guest Wi-Fi, with no password, and a log-on screen that needs participant email information.
- Guest Wi-Fi, with no password, and a log-on screen that requires a pre-assigned individual code. **Hardest to use.**

As a trainer you do not want to spend 15 minutes waiting and helping each of your participants to log on to the internet; if you have 30 participants on your course you have just lost a day's productivity between everyone.

Give participants a device

A final solution to promote independent study at your training is to have laptops or tablet computers for each participant (or pair) that you can lend out on the day. This can work particularly well if there is a particular piece of software that everybody needs access to, or if there is a set of files that everybody needs shared access to. Do check before the participants arrive that every device is logging on, is able to access the internet and is charged up. To help look after this equipment, you can often buy 'ruggedised' (hard-wearing or shock-resistant) cases to protect them.

Table 5.2 Recommended readings and resources

Source	Title	Author/s	Year	Web link
Website	Use keyboard shortcuts to deliver your presentation	support.office.com	2016	http://tinyurl.com/jafshgz

References

Becta (2007). *Case study: visualisers.* Available at: http://dera.ioe.ac.uk/1498/1/becta_2007_wholeclass teaching_visualisers_report.pdf (accessed 1 November, 2016).

CDW (2016). *Bring your own device. Preparing for the influx of mobile computing devices in schools.* Available at: www.edtechmagazine.com/k12/sites/default/files/111331-w-k12-byod-df.pdf (accessed 1 November, 2016).

support.office.com (2016). *Use keyboard shortcuts to deliver your presentation.* Available at: https://support.office.com/en-gb/article/Use-keyboard-shortcuts-to-deliver-your-presentation-1524ffce-bd2a-45f4-9a7f-f18b992b93a0 (accessed 1 November, 2016).

Learning phase 3

Embedding the learning and developing the participant

Chapter 6

Talk

> **Simon says:**
>
> " I remember attending a training session once where the trainer said that they had a simple rule: 19 minutes of input and then activity. This has always stuck with me because when I started training I was very conscious of ensuring that I followed this rule. As time has gone on I recognise that I now do about 12–15 minutes of input and then let participants talk. I do this to ensure that participants do not get used to the sound of my voice (my dulcet Yam Yam tones!) but I also see it as a way of getting participants to interact with each other, reflecting on what has been shared with them so that they can ask questions, compare their understanding and situate the input into some kind of context, this typically being their professional role and their classroom. As participants talk I like to circulate around the training room and 'earwig' – this allows me to listen in to different conversations so that I can check they are actually talking about what they should be talking about (!) and identify any misconceptions. I think it is important for participants to talk not just to those either side of them but to others on different tables and to have time to talk to me – that is why I promote 'active talking' where participants have to physically move around whilst conversing with others to get different viewpoints and ideas. "

When we talk about 'talk' what are we actually talking about?! The Department for Education and Skills (2007) asserts that 'talk' is synonymous with 'speaking' and 'spoken language'; this differs to oracy or oral communication where the emphasis is placed on speaking and listening. Whilst the importance of listening cannot be underestimated (see Van Duzer, 1997), our interest is focussed more on the 'distinctive features' of talk. These include:

1 Who is talking?
2 What is being talked about?
3 What kinds of talk are taking place (Department for Education and Skills, 2003) when planning, delivering and evaluating training sessions to improve participant learning?

Effective practice calls on trainers to be mindful of a simple rule: you should do more of the listening and participants should do more of the talking (adapted from Trevelyan, 2014: 257). But why should this be the case? We argue that there is a place for trainers to 'talk more', especially when they are introducing a concept, idea, theory or strategy to participants. However, there is a danger that this presenter talk or 'instructor talk' (Seidel *et al.*, 2015) can saturate whole training sessions. Thus, in an effort to maintain participants' attention levels, there should be planned/impromptu opportunities for them to talk, not only with those next to them or on their working table, but also with participants from other tables and with the trainer. These opportunities could/should occur prior to, during and after the training that is delivered, when appropriate.

There is a danger that trainers see talk as a simple classroom management strategy that helps to keep participants 'on task'. Alexander, however, passionately highlights 'the six vital functions of classroom talk' in primary and secondary schools, these being 'for *thinking, learning, communicating, democratic engagement, teaching* and *assessing*' (2012: 4, original emphasis). We feel that all of these functions resonate strongly with the adult training context, especially learning, for it is Vella (1994) who suggests that adults learn best when they are engaged in dialogue with others.

There is much evidence to support Vella's assertion (see, for example, Avoseh, 2005), particularly when the thinking of Vygotsky (1978) is taken into consideration. He theorised learning as a social process, arguing that knowledge is constructed in the midst of our interactions with others. The benefits of these interactions include the development of one's 'language – which supports thinking' along with 'provid[ing] feedback and assistance that support on-going learning' (Darling-Hammond *et al.*, 2003: 126). Trainers who subscribe to Vygotsky's social constructivist theory are likely to ask participants thought-provoking, open-ended questions to facilitate discussion (Reed and Koliba, 1995), along with creating 'safe' learning environments or spaces in which participants are encouraged and feel secure enough to be able to express and explore their thoughts, feelings and emotions as part of their 'learning journey' (Mooney, 2011).

It is within these 'safe' learning environments (typically the training classroom) that participants can use talk as a way of exploring their own learning needs (participant-led) rather than their anticipated or 'expected' needs (trainer-led). Cole *et al.* (2007: 7) propose a learning process that provides a useful structure for us to consider possible subject content or topics/activities which help to give 'training talk' a focus; this is offered in Table 6.1.

Table 6.1 Cole *et al.*'s (2007) adapted learning process and associated talk foci

Learning process (adapted from Cole *et al.* 2007)	Talk focus (examples)
Experience: Participants actively engage in an activity that involves them talking with others.	Discussing the content of a case study. Debating possible solutions for a scenario-based problem.
Reflection: Participants reflect on the experience to identify what it means to them.	Sharing personal/professional thinking. Comparing experiences with others.
Learning: As a result of the experience and the reflection, participants have increased self-awareness and can plan how they might improve their provision and practice.	Explaining what has been learned to others, e.g. colleagues, peers, members of the senior management team. Identifying targets for action. Evaluating the impact of planned actions.

You are likely to note in Table 6.1 a number of 'action verbs' that shape the focus of talk, e.g. discussing and explaining. These mirror those found in Bloom's Revised Taxonomy (Anderson and Krathwohl, 2001) as they help to suggest different kinds of talk that can be promoted in training sessions. We strongly believe that effective trainers think more about the kinds of talk they want participants to utilise, planning activities that will yield these within the training classroom as opposed to planning activities and then thinking about the kinds of talk it will promote. By doing this, you are able to engage participants in a balanced suite of 'doing talk' in an effort to purposefully facilitate learning (Fisher and Frey, 2008). But, as Zhang (2009) argues, various kinds of talk are unlikely to contribute equally to learning.

Dawes *et al.* (n.d.: 2) present what they refer to as a three-part typology of talk, emphasising that exploratory talk – 'in which [adults] engage critically but constructively with each other's ideas' – is deemed to 'improve the educational quality of ... collaborative activity and talk'. This is in opposition to disputational talk ('characterized by disagreement and individualized decision making') or cumulative talk ('characterized by repetitions, confirmations and elaborations'). To that end, you are actively encouraged to promote the characteristics or 'features' of exploratory talk as identified by Neil Mercer (quoted in National Literacy Trust, 2012: 2) in your training through active modelling, and the verbal/written sharing of 'the rules of talk' to aid participants' engagement with this type of talk and the learning which results from this. There are other types of talk available for trainers to use to facilitate participant learning, examples of which include dialogic talk (Alexander, 2008) and Socratic talk (see Ross, 2003), each with their own merits and limitations. Dialogic talk refers to both trainers and participants making 'substantial and significant [verbal] contributions ... through which [participants'] thinking on a given idea or theme is helped to move forward' (Mercer, 2003: 74); Socratic talk, on the other hand, is defined as 'talking about talk', used as a reflective tool so participants can decide if their discussion has been productive/accurate/etc. You are encouraged to engage with the recommended follow-up readings offered in Table 6.2 if you wish to explore one of these types of talk further.

In summary:

- Talk can improve the learning of participants in your training sessions.
- There are many ways we can structure activities to encourage the different types of talk that are required to deepen participants' understanding.

Table 6.2 Recommended readings and resources

Source	Title	Author/s	Year	Web link
Summary paper	Dialogic teaching essentials	Alexander	2010	http://tinyurl.com/lsfm69q
Short thesis	The Socratic method as an approach to learning and its benefits	Lam	2011	http://tinyurl.com/o66u5u4
Workshop pack	Helping adults learn (see *Discussion Methods*, pp. 34-63)	Brookfield	2011	http://tinyurl.com/n5rvbr3

Thought tunnel

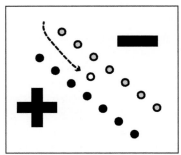

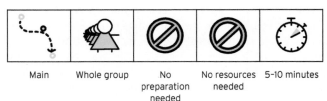

| Main | Whole group | No preparation needed | No resources needed | 5-10 minutes |

Thought tunnel (sometimes called 'Conscience alley') is a wonderful strategy that we have adapted from drama circles. Organise participants from the training group into two straight lines that are facing each other, with a sufficient gap so that one participant (Participant X) can easily walk down between the two lines that represent the sides of 'the tunnel'. Give each line time to think about and discuss amongst themselves an idea, a theory, a piece of knowledge, a strategy or a dilemma - one line should consider the **pros** whilst the other line considers the **cons**. As Participant X walks down the tunnel they should hear the verbalised thoughts of each line, the pros in one ear and the cons in the other; at the end of the tunnel they decide which viewpoint/decision/thinking was most persuasive.

Benefits
- Thought Tunnel actively encourages exploratory talk to enable participants to deepen their understanding of a situation, a concept, a viewpoint or an approach.
- Thought Tunnel not only helps participants to consider and voice differing viewpoints but it also promotes attentive listening skills.

Considerations
- Ensure that there is sufficient space in the training space to create the 'tunnel' - use a straight corridor if necessary.
- Place the strongest/keenest participants towards the end of the tunnel.
- Participants who lack confidence can take part by 'passing', e.g. by clapping or repeating a comment that has already been verbalised.

Set-up tips
- As the trainer, you should manage the activity from the outside of the tunnel, encouraging Participant X to move through the tunnel slowly; only the participants that they are 'in line with' should speak.

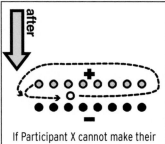

If Participant X cannot make their mind up encourage them to walk back through the tunnel again but with the pro and con sides swapped.

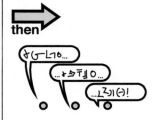

Encourage the 'lined' participants to improve their arguments by building on what the previous person in their line has said.

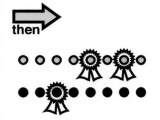

Ask the participant to choose and explain which of the statements, from either the pros or cons, was the most persuasive.

Cross cutting

Organise participants into two groups. Get the groups to 'play out' a scene in which a recently discussed idea or strategy is applied to a work-based context. Arrange it so that these scenes are played out at the same time. Video this and then play it back to the participants, discussing which scene highlights the strengths or limitations of the idea/strategy more effectively.

Extension – Get participants to talk about and then revise their scene to aid a deeper understanding of the idea/approach being advocated.

Flashback/flash forwards

Invite participants to talk about and then 'bring to life' (through words and movement) their thinking about what may have occurred that required a particular strategy/idea/suggestion (flashback) and what might happen after this strategy had been utilised (flash forwards) to help them think critically about cause and effect.

Alternative – Get participants to talk about alternative 'flash forwards' if the strategy/idea/suggestion was adapted in some way.

Shining a spotlight

Give participants a case study, a vignette or a scenario on paper. Offer them laser pointers or small torches for them to literally 'shine a spotlight' on an aspect of the text they have been given. Discuss its significance and how aspects of the 'spotlight text' could be altered in response to new knowledge acquired by participants from the training.

Alternative – Get participants to 'shine a spotlight' on their own professional experiences, making links to the case study/vignette/scenario they have been given.

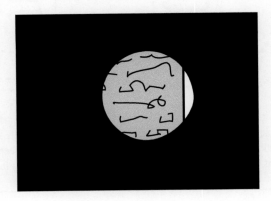

Walkie-talkie

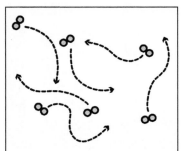

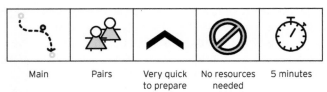

| Main | Pairs | Very quick to prepare | No resources needed | 5 minutes |

Give participants an opportunity to 'talk and walk' (discuss something whilst 'stretching their legs') during the training session. Promote purposeful talk by asking participants to reflect on their professional practice, discuss a new idea/piece of research, or share their learning from the session to date. Randomly pair up participants using names from a hat, or based upon specialisms or experience. Invite all pairs to circulate around the room at the same time, talking **only to their partner** as they walk. As participants move you can monitor the discussions of the different pairs to pick up on any issues or misconceptions. At the end of the activity invite individuals to share points raised from their paired discussions with those on their working tables.

Benefits
- This strategy helps to promote purposeful talk and an opportunity for physical activity.
- This strategy effectively energises the engagement levels of participants during a training session.

Considerations
- With some pairs you may want to deepen their talk using various question stems, e.g. where and when.
- Offer participants stems such as 'How do you know…?' or 'Why do you think that…?' verbally or on small cue cards as they move around the room.

Set-up tips
- Sufficient space is needed for pairs to be able to move about without bumping into chairs/tables/each other. If the training room is small consider using alternative spaces, e.g. corridors, a spare training room or the car park (weather permitting).

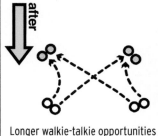

Longer walkie-talkie opportunities can be facilitated by asking pairs to 'split and re-pair' with a different participant.

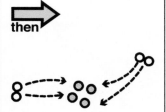

Pairs can combine to form a group of four, with individuals sharing the thoughts of their partner with the small group.

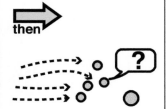

Invite individual participants to identify any misconceptions or follow-on questions for trainer clarification with the whole group.

Random microphone

Get a small group of participants to pick up an object to represent the random microphone, e.g. a bottle of water or a pen. Tell participants what to talk about, e.g. a scenario, a strategy or a concept. Participants should be encouraged to contribute to the discussion but can only do so if they are physically passed the microphone and are holding it.

   Alternative – Invite participants to stand in a small circle. They can only talk if they are standing in the middle of the circle (and only one person is allowed in at a time).

Silent speakers

Organise participants into small groups. Focus their talk on a case study, an extract from an article or a role play situation. Invite one participant in the group to articulate their thoughts/ideas/opinions but without speaking, relying on the mouthing of words, facial gestures and physical body movements to convey meaning. Another participant is to observe the 'silent speaker' and interpret their thoughts/ideas/opinions by verbalising them for the benefit of the remaining participants. Once finished, the 'silent speaker' should clarify their thoughts/ideas/opinions verbally.

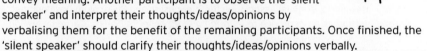

   Alternative – Participants may take digital images of the 'silent speaker' and invite participants from other groups to interpret their thoughts/ideas/opinions.

Talking cake mix

Get participants to sit in a circle, telling each participant they are a cake ingredient, e.g. flour, sugar, eggs, butter. Give participants a topic for purposeful talk, e.g. evaluate a video, discuss the content of a handout or verbalise a small plan of action. Call out one of the cake ingredients so that those people all have to swap seats within the circle. Get alternative participants to then talk to the person to the left of them about the talking topic. Shout out 'Cake Mix!' to change the seating position of all participants. Get alternative participants to then talk to the person to the right of them.

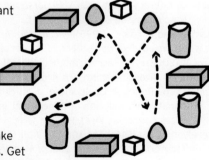

References

Alexander, R. (2008). *Towards Dialogic Teaching: Rethinking Classroom Talk*, 4th edn. York: Dialogos.
Alexander, R. (2010). *Dialogic teaching essentials*. Unpublished paper. Available at: www.serwis.wsjo.pl/lektor/1316/FINAL%20Dialogic%20Teaching%20Essentials.pdf (accessed 21 May, 2017).
Alexander, R. (2012). *Improving oracy and classroom talk in English schools: Achievements and challenges*. Available at: http://tinyurl.com/q4d3znz (accessed 25 October, 2015).

Anderson, L. W. and Krathwohl, D. R. (2001). *A Taxonomy for Learning, Teaching, and Assessing*, abridged edn. Boston: Allyn and Bacon.

Avoseh, M. B. M. (2005). The power of voice: An analysis of dialogue as a method in both elementary and adult education. *International Journal of Case Method Research & Application*, 17(3), 374-384.

Brookfield, S. (2011). *Helping adults learn*. Workshop, University of St Thomas, Minneapolis. Available at: http://tinyurl.com/n5rvbr3 (accessed 21 May, 2017).

Cole, D., Ellis, C., Mason, B., Meed, J., Record, D., Rossetti, A. and Willcocks, G. (2007). *Teaching speaking and listening: a toolkit for practitioners*. London: Department of Education and Skills. Available at: www3.canisius.edu/~justice/CSTmodule-final/Teaching%20speaking%20and%20listening%20a%20 toolkit%20for%20practitioners.pdf (accessed 23 April, 2017).

Darling-Hammond, L., Austin, K., Orcutt, S. and Martin, D. with contributions from Tharp, R. and Palincsar, A. (2003). *Learning from others: Learning in a social context*. Stanford, CA: Stanford University School of Education.

Dawes, L., Littleton, K., Mercer, N., Wegerif, R. and Warwick, P. (n.d.). *Thinking together in the primary classroom*. Milton Keynes: CREET, The Open University. Available at: http://tinyurl.com/qaa7aax (accessed 26 October, 2015).

Department for Education and Skills (2003). *Speaking, Listening, Learning: Working with Children in Key Stages 1 and 2*. Norwich: HMSO. Available at: http://tinyurl.com/br7dgmt (accessed 25 October, 2015).

Department for Education and Skills (2007). *Improving Speaking and Listening Skills: A Practical Guide for Skills for Life Teachers*. Nottingham: DfES Publications. Available at: http://tinyurl.com/ouh3xt2 (accessed 25 October, 2015).

Fisher, D. and Frey, N. (2008). *Better Learning Through Structured Teaching: A Framework for the Gradual Release of Responsibility*. Alexandria, Virginia: Association for Supervision and Curriculum Development.

Lam, F. (2011). *The Socratic method as an approach to learning and its benefits*. Thesis, Carnegie Mellon University.

Mercer, N. (2003). The educational value of 'dialogic talk' in 'whole-class dialogue'. In: Qualifications and Curriculum Authority, *New Perspectives on Spoken English in the Classroom: Discussion Papers* (pp. 73-76). London: Qualifications and Curriculum Authority. Available at: http://tinyurl.com/qbb6uw5 (accessed 4 November, 2015).

Mooney, D. (2011). Charting the learning journey of a group of adults returning to education. *Adult Learner 2011: The Irish Journal of Adult and Community Education*, 126-144.

National Literacy Trust (2012). *Understanding different types of talk*. Available at: http://tinyurl.com/ njdso6o (accessed 26 October, 2015).

Reed, J. and Koliba, C. (1995). *Facilitating Reflection: A Manual for Leaders and Educators*. Available at: www.uvm.edu/~dewey/reflect.pdf (accessed 26 October, 2015).

Ross, V. (2003). The Socratic method: What it is and how to use it in the classroom. *Speaking of Teaching*, 13(1), 1-4. Available at: http://tinyurl.com/nrxjzpp (accessed 26 October, 2015).

Seidel, S. B., Reggi, A. L., Schinske, J. N., Burrus, L. W. and Tanner, K. D. (2015). Beyond the biology: A systematic investigation of noncontent instructor talk in an introductory biology course. *CBE: Life Sciences Education*, 14(4), 1-14.

Trevelyan, J. P. (2014). *The Making of an Expert Engineer: How to Have a Wonderful Career Creating a Better World and Spending Lots of Money Belonging to Other People*. Leiden: CRC Press/Balkema.

Van Duzer, C. (1997). Promoting education and achievement of adults learning English. *CALSolutions*, February. Available at: http://tinyurl.com/p7shqv3 (accessed 25 October, 2015).

Vella, J. (1994). *Learning to Listen, Learning to Teach: The Power of Dialogue in Educating Adults*. San Francisco: Jossey-Bass Publisher.

Vygotsky, L. S. (1978). *Mind in Society: The Development of Higher Psychological Processes*. Cambridge, MA: Harvard University Press.

Zhang, Y. (2009). Classroom discourse and student learning. *Asian Social Science*, 4(9), 80-83. Available at: http://tinyurl.com/nmpkoup (accessed 26 October, 2015).

Snapshot F: Managing participant behaviour

It may seem a little strange to see a Snapshot about managing the behaviour of participants; after all, adults know how to behave, right?! Surprisingly, based on our experiences of training adults and mentoring other trainers, this is not necessarily the case. There may be times when you encounter adult behaviours that you normally associate with those exhibited by children, e.g. shouting, arguing, sighing, doodling and sleeping! Good trainers do not assume that all participants will behave appropriately in their training (although the vast majority of them will), so it is good practice to have a wealth of practical strategies to hand so that the behaviour of certain individuals does not interfere with the learning which takes place during your training. We advocate the use of the 'Be Clear' approach (Brownhill in Shelton and Brownhill, 2008: 40) as this offers three simple steps to help professionals effectively address behavioural difficulties:

1 **Be clear** about what you see – do you know what behaviour you are observing? Can you define it?
2 **Be clear** about what is causing it – what factors are influencing this behaviour?
3 **Be clear** about what you are going to do about it – what strategies do you intend to put in place to manage the behaviour observed? Why have you selected these strategies?

With this approach in mind, we offer a summary table (Table 6.3) that identifies a select number of adult behaviours that you are likely to come across when you are training. We will consider some of the influencing factors (*Possible reasoning*) for these behaviours, and practical ways (*Useful strategies*) in which these behaviours can be managed during a training session.

Table 6.3 Participant behaviours, possible influences and effective management strategies

Behaviour	Possible reasoning	Useful strategies
Reluctance to engage in group activities	▪ Participant is tired. ▪ Participant is nervous or anxious. ▪ Participant is unaware of or does not appreciate the benefits of collaborating with others.	▪ Invite participants to take a 'lead role' when undertaking group activities. ▪ Offer participants specific verbal encouragement and non-verbal support, e.g. thumbs up or a smile. ▪ Plan for participants to undertake paired work with someone they know, as and where appropriate.
Dominant participant	▪ Participant is overcompensating – they feel as if they have to 'prove themselves'. ▪ It is their natural disposition. ▪ Participant is trying to impress either you as the trainer or others.	▪ Direct oral/written questions to different individuals/groups as part of your taught input. ▪ Provide a 'Contributor Ball' (inflatable globe, for example) that can be passed (thrown) around the room at different times during the session – whoever is holding it is the only person who can talk/answer questions. ▪ Politely encourage the dominant participant to 'Give others a chance!' ▪ Ask them to write questions down on a notepad for consideration later.

Table 6.3 Continued

Behaviour	Possible reasoning	Useful strategies
Talking to others when you are delivering	Participant is trying to relieve boredom (think: how long have you been talking at them for?). Participant wants to clarify a training point with a peer. Participant is talking about work-related issues with their colleagues.	Plan frequent opportunities for participants to talk to others with a specific learning purpose. Politely ask everyone in the training room to listen when you are talking (this should be done at the very start of the training session). Occasionally catch the eye of the participant, or wait if necessary to gain the attention of the distracting individual.
Participant who texts, takes phone calls, or who surfs the internet during taught input	Participant is trying to keep on top of the demands of their day job. Participant is dealing with personal difficulties. Participant is following up training points made during your taught input.	Encourage all participants to put their phones away or switch them to silent during direct training time. Quietly have a word with individuals who are constantly distracted or distract others with their phone/laptop/tablet. Build moments into your training for participants to quickly check their phones or use the internet (we call these 'Mobile Moments').
The participant who 'knows-it-all'	Participant has already engaged in training related to the training focus. It could be a mindset issue – the participant does not appreciate the value of the training focus for their professional role. Participant is trying to hide some underlying personal insecurities.	Offer opportunities for participants to share their knowledge and experience with their working tables or the whole group (specific time limits are needed!). Encourage participants to see how your training supports, challenges or extends what they already know. Give participants a listening role during group activities, quickly feeding back to you in written note form to help shape some of your taught input (what do participants still not understand or have misconceptions about?). If you know in advance there are participants who are likely to be an issue, arrange group work with 'know-it-alls' acting as mentors. Give the mentors a special role to perform, such as 'Here is what I'm trying to teach, try to help the group discussion reach these conclusions without having to tell them'.

Strategies for managing participant behaviour will not work equally well with all individuals or groups. There are, however, a number of ideas that the training community consider to be consistently effective in helping to manage adult behaviour:

1   Invite participants to discuss and share what **their** expectations of **you** are, e.g. be polite, respectful of everyone's contributions, actively listen to others and be encouraging. How similar are these to the behaviours that you expect of them?

2 'Look for the good' by working hard to spot participants attentively listening, taking notes, asking questions and participating, thanking them privately or publicly for their engagement and contributions.

3 Offer participants variety to sustain their interest in the training you deliver, e.g. speed up or slow down the pace, facilitate time for group discussion/reflection, plan for an activity or move the learning to a different part of the room (a different table, a circle of chairs or the floor).

4 Never underestimate the power of body language in managing participant behaviour – think about the messages you can quickly convey with a smile, a stare, holding your hand up, clapping, folding your arms or not moving at all.

5 Provide incentives for behaviours exhibited by participants that they have collaboratively agreed on, e.g. allowing them to go for coffee five minutes earlier, giving them opportunities to check their phones/work email, or providing them with a selection of sweets or sticky stars (Alan loves receiving these!) as part of an afternoon 'reward'/pick-me-up.

Table 6.4 Recommended readings and resources

Source	Title	Author/s	Year	Web link
Blog	Dealing with troublesome adult learners in the classroom	Albrecht	2013	http://tinyurl.com/y8scymh7
Professional guide	Classroom management	UCU	n.d.	http://tinyurl.com/zaf2dhq

References

Shelton, F. and Brownhill, S. (2008). *Effective Behaviour Management in the Primary School*. Maidenhead: Open University Press.

University and College Union (n.d.). *Classroom management*. London: University and College Union. Available at: http://tinyurl.com/zaf2dhq (accessed 22 May, 2017).

Chapter 7
Engaging with texts

Alan says:

" I'm going to make an admission. Once I went to some training and I had not done the requisite pre-course reading. Well, OK, maybe more than once. However, when I've been given a piece of text on the day to read I have always read it, and then enjoyed any discussion around it afterwards. However, just two weeks ago I heard a tale from a teacher who described the worst training she had ever attended which started with her being given twenty minutes to do a reading, most of which was just supporting the main point and not actually stating something new. Getting that balance between the length of reading, the time allowed and sufficiently in-depth content is the trick in getting participants to engage successfully with readings. If you get it wrong, you are more likely to be punished for it when working with adults, than with children (see Snapshot L).

Jeff Bezos, the founder, chairman and chief executive officer of Amazon reportedly starts his meetings with time to independently read and digest six-page memos in silence, before they interview the author of the memos in great detail. This tells us two things: giving participants time to read and make their own conclusions is a good thing; however, the preparation of the memos must also be incredibly thorough, so we need to be strict when preparing/choosing/ editing suitable readings. **"**

In 1992 Fleming and Mills reported on their research involving learners 'reflecting upon their sensory modality preferences' (1992: 137). By this they were referring to the ways learners learned information. Fleming and Mills' article launched VARK, an acronym which stands for Visual, Aural, Read/write, and Kinaesthetic sensory modalities. The focus of this chapter introduction is on the third modality – Read/write – with a particular emphasis on reading. Whilst there has been much criticism about learning styles from academic circles, we support Fleming's assertion that '[n]ot much [criticism] comes from those who use learning styles as part of their strategies for learning, training and teaching' (Fleming 2012: 1). Indeed, we consider reading to be an important component of good training because it not only helps to develop participants' minds but also improves their focus and concentration, promotes the discovery of new things, and, interestingly, helps to relieve stress if undertaken for just six minutes (see Lewis, 2009). Simple opportunities for reading to be facilitated during your training might include:

- Participants reading the professional article you have set them as a Prior Reading Task before attending the training day.
- Participants reading the bullet points presented on the PowerPoint slides that are being used to structure your taught input.
- Participants reading the case studies that are offered in the handout materials you have prepared to supplement and enhance the training experience.
- Participants reading the information found on websites you have recommended that they browse through before, during or after the training session.

One of the challenges you are likely to face is getting participants to actually read and digest the text that is offered to them. This may come as a surprise to some of you; after all, aren't we dealing with adults here? In our experience, we have encountered participants who use 'reading time' as an opportunity to simply stare at the page (no eye movements to track the sentences) without processing the text. Even worse, there are those who engage in a whispered conversation with a peer, those who have a quick look at the messages on their phone, or those who choose to do some 'real' work! So how can this be positively addressed? The answer is by getting participants to **engage** with the text.

Engaging with a text

We first need to be clear about what we mean by 'engagement'. Whilst there is no fixed, universal definition, the term (in our mind) suggests activity. Trowler builds on this, proposing that 'engagement is more than [just] involvement or participation – it requires feelings and sense-making as well as activity' (2010: 5). This clearly reflects the definition of engagement proposed by Fredricks, Blumenfeld and Paris (2004: 62–63) who identify three dimensions to student engagement. These are presented and briefly explained in Table 7.1 in the context of adult learners, along with associated characteristics exhibited by participants when they are 'engaged with a text'.

Table 7.1 Positive characteristics displayed by participants when engaging with text (adapted from Lester, 2013: 7)

Dimension	Explanation	Associated 'reading' characteristics
Behavioural	Participants' engagement in the learning activity	'Rules' of the activity are followed, e.g. silent reading. Full concentration is directed to the actual text. Attention is focussed on the meaning of the text. Persistence is utilised to read on to the end of the text. Effort is made to reflect critically on the text content. Questions are asked to clarify meaning/misunderstanding. Contributions are willingly made to verbal discussions.
Emotional	Participants' reactions (affective and emotional) to the learning activity	Genuine interest in the text is expressed (be it verbally and/or through facial expressions). The physical 'act' of reading the text is enjoyed (noted through visual cues). Participants are happy to share their thoughts about the text with others in verbal/written form. Feelings toward the trainer are positive (despite the fact they have been asked by them to read something!). Participants feel a sense of belonging and importance when engaged in a reading activity in the training environment.
Cognitive	Participants' psychological engagement in the learning activity	Participants are motivated to learn something new from the text. They are thoughtful in their responses to the text. Effort is made to comprehend complex ideas discussed in the text. Participants are clearly invested in the reading activity to enhance their learning. They relish the challenge offered by academic texts. Participants are able to make connections between theory and practice.

An appreciation of the different ways we can tell when participants are truly engaged with their reading enables us to promote these characteristics through the tasks we set and the feedback we give. Ways in which these characteristics can be actively encouraged include:

- Asking participants to verbally identify characteristics they think you are looking for when they are engaged with the text – why are they important?
- Challenging participants to demonstrate certain characteristics before they engage with the text, e.g. silent (focussed) reading.
- Offering verbal/non-verbal praise to participants as they demonstrate certain character-istics while they engage with the text, e.g. quietly thanking a table for their efforts to read in silence.
- Actively encouraging participants to model certain characteristics whilst they engage with the text, e.g. annotating the text as opposed to just highlighting it.
- Getting participants to self-assess themselves against a list of 'engaged' characteristics that are presented on a PowerPoint slide or on a bookmark after their engagement with the text, e.g. have you generated a question to stimulate discussion about the reading?

But we still need to know how to effectively engage participants with texts that they read. Unfortunately, there are is no 'one way' by which this can be achieved. You should make an informed decision about the strategies you would like to use in your own training based on the participants that you are working with and their particular needs. To that end, a suite of general and specific strategies is offered in Table 7.2 for you to 'pick and choose' from that complement and validate ideas in the remainder of this chapter.

Table 7.2 Considerations and techniques to help participants engage with text

Make sure you give participants something interesting to actually read, content-wise!	Offer participants a choice of texts to read so that they feel in control of their learning.
Allow participants to access texts in different formats, e.g. printed, electronic and oral readings on a CD.	Give participants a key question to which you would like the answer. Get participants to read the text with the key question 'in mind'.
Suggest that participants try to reduce the content of the text read into a Tweet (made up of a 140-letter character limit).	As they read, get participants to create a Text Map that presents the main ideas as 'points of interest'.
Invite participants to read parts of their text out loud to a peer; if the peer is able to recall three pieces of information then the participants can swap roles.	Challenge participants to make mental connections with the text they are reading and the training content they have engaged with to date.
Get participants to engage with their text in different places in the training room and at different levels (standing, sitting at a table, lying on the floor), alternating these as they read.	Suggest that participants take on the role of a salesperson who circulates around the training room, verbally 'selling' the content of their recently read text to others as part of a two-minute challenge!
Give participants two pieces of L-shaped paper that can be arranged as a viewfinder to help them focus on a significant sentence/small paragraph for others to read and pass comment on.	Organise participants into reading groups of around four, who each have the same text. Assign a section for each of them to read and discuss in order to effectively reduce solitary reading time.

Table 7.2 Continued

Get participants to read and reflect on a text that you have personally written. Facilitate an opportunity for them to 'Argue with the Author' over any controversial points you have made.	Invite participants to use the classic '3-2-1' strategy to summarise the text they have read:
	▢ write down 3 things you have found out;
	▢ make a note of 2 things that interest you;
	▢ jot down 1 question you still have.

In summary:

▢ Reading is an important strategy that promotes learning.
▢ Engagement is more than just 'activity'.
▢ Trainers should be mindful of the three dimensions of engagement when promoting associated 'engaged' reading characteristics.
▢ Engagement with a text can occur before, during and after it has been read.

Table 7.3 Recommended readings and resources

Source	Title	Author/s	Year	Web link
Short book	Engaging Adult Learners: Philosophy, Principles and Practices	Bryson	2013	http://tinyurl.com/zqpg94h
Article*	103 things to do before/during/after reading	Burke	2015	http://tinyurl.com/mpnuux8
Online* PDF	How to actively engage students through creative approaches to reading in lessons	National Literacy Trust	n.d.	http://tinyurl.com/jzv2274

* Suggestions made in this article/online PDF can be easily adapted for the adult training context and applied to non-fiction texts.

Annotating text

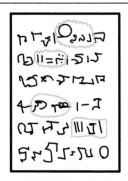

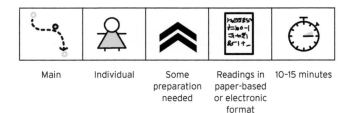

Main | Individual | Some preparation needed | Readings in paper-based or electronic format | 10-15 minutes

Many of your participants will be familiar with the basic idea of highlighting text that they read but this is unlikely to actually help them learn very much. Instead, if you want them to engage more deeply and critically with the readings that you offer, think about showing them different ways to record their engagement with the text through written means. This includes the use of underlining, drawing different shapes around key ideas, theories or strategies, using arrows ▼▲ to identify connections between ideas, or offering symbols to indicate things that they do not understand, e.g. ?, *, [ ] or #. Offer participants time after their reading/annotation to discuss their thoughts with others.

Benefits
- Annotating texts helps to focus the attention of participants and develop levels of concentration.
- As a strategy, it provides participants with an immediate self-check of their understanding of the key ideas contained within a text.

Considerations
- You should help participants by providing them with succinct readings that are accessible in terms of their writing tone, vocabulary choices, theoretical/practical content and relevance to the training focus.

Set-up tips
- Present different ways of annotating text on separate sheets of large paper around the training room so that participants have a visual reference point to support them and a choice as to how they could engage with the text.
- Offer participants a range of stationary in the form of pencils, coloured pens, rulers and sticky labels to help them with their annotating.

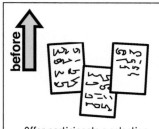

Offer participants a selection of readings to choose from and annotate by summarising important ideas in their own words.

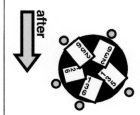

Invite small groups of participants to collate their summarised ideas together, identifying the most salient points.

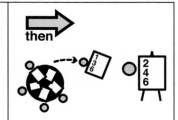

Share the ideas that you thought were most important in the reading, and nominate a spokesperson from each group to compare their conclusions with yours.

Verbalised annotation

Invite one participant to read aloud sections of the reading that you would like the whole group to engage with. Suggest that the remaining participants listen carefully, following along by silently reading the text and annotating it with marginal notes between pauses in the verbalised reading.

Alternative - Invite participants to read aloud for their working table only, annotating the text with relevant questions.

Noted annotations

Challenge participants to record their annotations of a given text on sticky notes. Encourage participants to then physic-ally move around the training room, discussing the text with others with reference to their sticky note annotations only. Use this as an opportunity to listen in to participants' conversations to identify any misconceptions, thus helping you to plan your next steps.

Alternative - Offer participants a choice of cue cards, envelopes, flash cards, playing cards or revision cards to record their annotations about things that they like or disagree with in the reading.

Quiz me!

Provide participants with a text for them to individually annotate using numbered bullet points ('Three key things I know now that I did not know before!'). Working in pairs, invite them to quiz each other about what they have read, discussing, reviewing, analysing, evaluating or critiquing the text through an engaging quiz: think 20 Questions, True or False, What's wrong with this statement? or Mastermind (their 'specialist subject' being the text).

Alternative - Invite participants to quiz you, the trainer, as a unique opportunity for them to gain an understanding of what you took from the reading and your thoughts about its implications for thinking and practice.

Making links

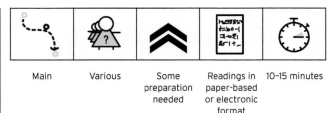

| Main | Various | Some preparation needed | Readings in paper-based or electronic format | 10–15 minutes |

When you offer participants readings in your training session, encourage them to make links between the ideas and thinking contained in the text with their own experiences and practices in the work setting. These connections can be suggested by you or the participants themselves prior to the reading, examples of which include links with other theories, concepts, strategies, themes, topics and skills. Alternatively, these could be formulated as participants read (individual/internally) or after they have read (through discussion/with others). These connections can be written down, discussed with peers/you, or included as part of a diagram.

Benefits	▧ Making links is considered to be a key strategy for supporting and developing participants' levels of comprehension and understanding.
	▧ This idea helps to 'emphasise ... a fusion of ideas and concepts' that can make training 'more relevant and meaningful' for all participants (Hayes, 2010: 383).
Considerations	▧ Participants may find it challenging at first, so you may need to model what you are expecting.
	▧ It is useful to give participants 'thinking time' (see Stahl, 1994) both during and after their engagement with the text.
Set-up tips	▧ Provide participants with sufficient paper and pens for them to jot down their connections as they read in an effort to capture and retain these for small group/whole group discussions.

Challenge participants to make links to other readings they have previously engaged with – think pre-course tasks, readings from other courses, professional articles, or readings undertaken as part of their personal studies.	Get participants to see if they can make any connections with the world in terms of policies in other countries or international practices that they are aware of.	Invite participants to share their links with others using group discussion techniques such as snowballing, jigsaws and envoys (see DfES, 2003: 4) to promote the verbal linking of ideas.

Visual linkage

Offer participants large sheets of paper (A3) onto which they can create flow charts, spider-diagrams, drawings, thought showers, grids, maps, concept maps, knowledge webs, tables or lists in an effort to visually record the links they have made with what they have read.

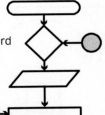

Alternative - Participants could try to decipher the links established by others via a Linkage Gallery in which the visual records are displayed for others to view and discuss.

Paper chain

Provide participants with coloured strips of paper and glue sticks. Get them to make a paper chain that physically presents the links they have made with what they have read. Model how to offer a link (in written form) on the outside of the paper link, ensuring that the chain is a connected mass of links rather than being a simple linear paper chain.

Alternative - Invite participants to work together on a collaborative paper chain, connecting links about the same reading or a different one (think *SOLO Taxonomy* - see http://tinyurl.com/jj748mm).

Questions for connection

Ask participants to organise themselves into small groups. Give each group a different reading, ensuring that each participant within the group has the same reading. Invite them to generate a series of questions that may help others to make links if/when they are offered their reading later on in the training session (if appropriate).

Alternative - Support participants in creating questions that promote different levels of thinking by completing the question stems offered by Bloom's Taxonomy Guide to Writing Questions (see http://tinyurl.com/d4pxm7s).

Skimming and scanning

| Main | Individual | Some preparation needed | Readings in paper-based or electronic format | 10–15 minutes |

Promote engagement with a purposeful reading by suggesting that they actively 'skim or scan' reading materials that you provide for them or that they bring with them to the training session; these could be in the form of newspaper clippings, professional articles, or extracts from reports or research papers. Suggest that they either 'skim' the reading to get the general idea or gist of the text, or 'scan' it by looking for specific information, e.g. keywords, phrases or names. Consider using a visual timer (see http://tinyurl.com/6tq73bu) to manage the amount of time the reading activity takes. Once participants have 'skimmed or scanned' their reading, invite them to share their learning/thoughts with others on their working table or as part of a whole group discussion.

Benefits
- Skimming and scanning encourages participants to read relevant but longer texts with a purpose, enabling them to focus on the main aims of the training session.
- These two reading strategies serve as valuable transferable skills that participants can actively use in their professional role when reading documents and looking at learners' work.

Considerations
- Clarify which terms or words you would like participants to 'hunt' for when scanning given texts.

Set-up tips
- Select readings that are easily accessible for participants in terms of their tone, writing style and vocabulary choices.

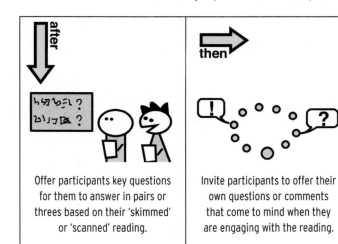

Offer participants key questions for them to answer in pairs or threes based on their 'skimmed' or 'scanned' reading.

Invite participants to offer their own questions or comments that come to mind when they are engaging with the reading.

Critique ideas or suggestions offered in the reading as part of a whole group discussion, thus creating useful opportunities for critical thought and debate.

Chain reading

Organise your participants into small reading groups. Offer them each a copy of the same reading (making sure it is more substantial in length), assigning each participant a small numbered paragraph/section of it. Once it has been read, invite Participant 1 to verbally summarise their paragraph/ section (number 1) as part of a group 'chain', followed by Participant 2 until all participants have spoken.

Alternative - Invite participants to decide on which sections of the reading they would like to focus on and verbally summarise as part of the group 'chain'.

Compare and contrast reading

Arrange the participants into seated pairs. Distribute two different readings so that each person in the pair has a different reading. Carefully select the readings so that they facilitate discussion and debate, e.g. one reading might positively promote something whereas the other reading may question its effectiveness. Give participants time to individually read their reading using skimming and scanning strategies, reflecting on what they have read and verbally sharing what their reading suggests with each other.

Follow-on - Invite participants to compare and contrast their own personal/professional thinking in relation to their assigned reading, verbalising this for the benefit of their partner.

Reading diet

Tell participants to take a reading on a weight-loss programme! Ask them to rewrite the reading first as three sentences, then as a single sentence. Finally ask them to reduce a whole reading into 10 or fewer words (they can compete with one another if they want). If you give them access to a computer to do this they can make edits and changes easily. The final 'reading' that participants produce is not actually as important as the process they go through; by asking participants to remove parts of the reading they will have to be critically reflective of it.

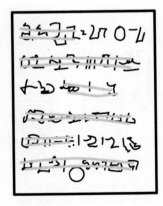

Alternative - Ask participants to cross out parts of the reading until only the key messages/words remain.

Slicing and dicing

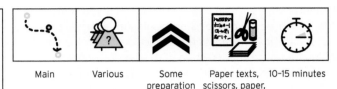

| Main | Various | Some preparation needed | Paper texts, scissors, paper, glue sticks | 10-15 minutes |

An effective way of getting participants to actively engage with texts in training sessions is to give them a pair of scissors and cut the text up (obviously there is a little more to it than just that!). For the activity to have purpose and meaning, it is a good idea for participants to have some idea about what they are 'slicing and dicing'; this might include keywords, essential ideas, significant findings, paragraphs of importance or crucial content. They then display their 'sliced and diced' information on pieces of paper to stimulate purposeful dialogue with their peers.

Benefits
- By reducing a reading down in terms of the amount of text that makes up the reading and what the text actually says, participants can effectively summarise the essence of a text for the benefit of themselves and others.
- As an activity, it provides participants with a purpose for reading and utilises a range of thinking skills when exploring the text, e.g. reasoning and evaluating.

Considerations
- You can help participants by providing them with succinct readings or extracts that are accessible in terms of their writing tone, vocabulary choices, theoretical/practical content and relevance to the training focus.

Set-up tips
- Prepare readings by using a large text size (size 16+) and providing suitable line spacing (1.5-2) to allow easy 'cutting access' to the text.
- Give participants large pieces of coloured paper to stick their 'sliced and diced' text on for display/discussion purposes.

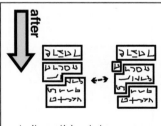

Invite participants to compare their 'sliced and diced' text with others who have read and cut up the same reading.

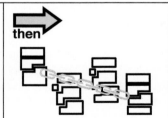

Think about organising participants in small groups and getting them to see if there are any connections between their 'sliced and diced' text in terms of similarities and differences in thinking, practice or understanding.

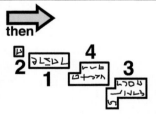

Working in small groups, participants rank their 'sliced and diced' text in terms of its significance, importance or relevance by numbering them.

Explanation explosion

Encourage participants to offer written comments, questions and thoughts around their 'sliced and diced' text in an effort to capture their personal/professional reflections about what they have selected.

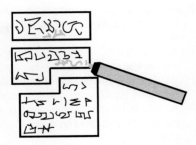

 Alternative - Promote the use of drawings, sketches, doodles, symbols or shapes as visual alternatives to represent participant reflections.

Transformation

Suggest that participants transform a reading by integrating it into an interesting text type idea (adapted from Petty, 2002: 6). This could include a leaflet, song lyrics, a report, a poem, a Twitter feed, or a set of instructions.

 Enrichment - For those text types that emphasise 'performance', e.g. chants, limericks and raps, you might encourage those participants who are willing to bring these to life with their voices and body movements!

Implications for thinking and practice

Challenge participants to think about the impact that their text could/should/will have on professional thinking and practice in the workplace. Provide them with arrow-shaped paper onto which they can write their ideas. Consider displaying these around the training room as an 'impact border' for participants to take digital images of and share with their work colleagues.

 Alternative - Invite participants to stand by the paper arrow which offers the most important impact (informed by 'sliced and diced' text) in terms of either shaping their thinking or influencing their impending practice. 'Which has had the greatest impact? Why?'

References

Bryson, J. D. (2013). *Engaging Adult Learners: Philosophy, Principles and Practices.* Barrie, Ontario: James David Bryson. Available at: http://northernc.on.ca/leid/docs/engagingadultlearners.pdf (accessed 22 May, 2017).

Burke, J. (2015). *103 things to do before/during/after reading.* Reading Rockets. Available at: http://tinyurl.com/mpnuux8 (accessed 22 May, 2017).

DfES (2003). *Group discussion and interaction: Making it work in the classroom.* Available at: www.babcock-education.co.uk/ldp/do_download.asp?did=301149 (accessed 23 April, 2017).

Fleming, N. D. (2012). *The case against learning styles: 'There is no evidence...'* Available at: http://vark-learn.com/wp-content/uploads/2014/08/The-Case-Against-Learning-Styles.pdf (accessed 4 August, 2016].

Fleming, N. D. and Mills, C. (1992). Not another inventory, rather a catalyst for reflection. *To Improve the Academy,* 11, 137–155.

Fredricks, J. A., Blumenfeld, P. C. and Paris, A. H. (2004). School engagement: Potential of the concept, state of the evidence. *Review of Educational Research,* 74(1), 59–109.

Hayes, D. (2010). The seductive charms of a cross-curricular approach. *Education 3-13: International Journal of Primary, Elementary and Early Years Education,* 38(4), 381–387.

Lester, D. (2013). A review of the student engagement literature. *Focus on Colleges, Universities, and Schools,* 7(1), 1–8. Available at: www.nationalforum.com/Electronic%20Journal%20Volumes/Lester,%20Derek%20A%20Review%20of%20the%20Student%20Engagement%20Literature%20FOCUS%20V7%20N1%202013.pdf (accessed 4 August, 2016).

Lewis, D. (2009). Reading 'can help reduce stress'. *Telegraph,* 30 March. Available at: www.telegraph.co.uk/news/health/news/5070874/Reading-can-help-reduce-stress.html (accessed 4 August, 2016).

National Literacy Trust (n.d.). *How to actively engage students through creative approaches to reading in lessons.* London: National Literacy Trust. Available at: http://tinyurl.com/jzv2274 (accessed 22 May, 2017).

Petty, G. (2002). *25 ways for teaching without talking: Presenting students with new material in theory lessons.* Available at: http://geoffpetty.com/wp-content/uploads/2012/12/25waysforTWT2.doc (accessed 16 November, 2015).

Stahl, R. J. (1994). *Using 'think-time' and 'wait-time' skilfully in the classroom.* Available at: http://files.eric.ed.gov/fulltext/ED370885.pdf (accessed 22 May, 2017).

Trowler, V. (2010). *Student engagement literature review.* York: The Higher Education Academy. Available at: www.heacademy.ac.uk/sites/default/files/studentengagementliteraturereview_1.pdf (accessed 4 August, 2016).

Snapshot G: Handouts

How many times have you attended training and come away from the session/day with a handout? We suspect that your answer is either 'Most of the time!' or 'Every time!' We know this because Wayne State University (n.d.: 1) asserts that handouts have become an 'integral component' when educating others to the point they are now just an expectation of training participants. Bligh offers a number of reasons as to why you should use handouts in your training (2000: 148-162); these have been adapted and are presented in Table 7.4, offering useful ideas about their possible content and how they might be used in training sessions:

Table 7.4 Reasons for using handouts and their possible content/usage as part of training sessions (adapted from Bligh, 2000)

Reason	Possible content/usage
Purpose	Handouts can be used to convey training aims, intentions/objectives and goals to participants.
Information	Handouts can help to ensure you: a) share with participants the same basic knowledge on which you will build new, related or more complex content b) save time by providing participants with valuable content that you are unable to present c) relieve some of the tension that participants often feel when they are presented with large amounts of new information.
Guide	Handouts can serve as a supportive guide to help participants navigate their way through difficult training material (think comprehensive charts, diagrams and images).
Sparing note-making	Some situations (think group activities) make it difficult for participants to take notes. Handouts may be created or distributed 'after-the-event', e.g. notes made by you that summarise a group discussion from the morning session.
Stimulate thought	Handouts that contain questions, quizzes or theoretical issues are useful to stimulate thought and fuel discussions/debates between participants.
Promote reading	Handouts can contain extracts from professional and academic sources (think articles, research papers and case studies) to nourish participants' subject knowledge and work-based practices. A recommended reading list could also be offered.

Based on our own experiences of being trained by others, we recognise a number of ways in which handouts can become an ineffective aspect of training delivery. These include:

1   'Death-by-handout' – Too many individual single-sheet handouts given out during the training session.
2   Distribution issues – Valuable training time wasted by trainers giving out handouts.
3   Presentation issues – Participants unable to read the printed text due to poor-quality photocopying or the text is not printed squarely on the page.
4   Order issues – Handouts are fastened together to form a 'training pack' but are not organised in the sequence that the training follows; no page numbers or contents page are offered to allow quick access to relevant handouts.

To positively address each of these issues, we offer you the following practical suggestions:

1 'Death-by-handout'
   - Be selective of the handouts you prepare.
   - Photocopy handouts on both sides of the paper.
   - Collate handouts together to create a 'training pack'.
2 Distribution issues
   - Give out all handouts at the start of the training session.
   - Or, distribute the next handout (face down) as participants engage with the current handout.
3 Presentation issues
   - Take time and care to ensure a high-quality presentation and printing of your handouts (see Yoshida, 2011 for some outstanding ideas).
4 Order issues
   - Ensure all handouts have page numbers or clear titles.
   - Organise the handouts in the order sequence of the content of the training/ presentation.

It is important to realise that there is no 'one way' to prepare, produce and use handouts for training purposes. With this in mind, we offer you a small collection of useful guidance, advice and suggestions via our 'Pick and Choose' box, thus allowing you to select the ideas that you would like to embrace as part of your own quality handout practice:

Pick and Choose – handouts!

- Think about the format you would like your handouts to be in, be they complete handouts (all of the training content) or incomplete ones (some of the training content missing).
- Consider presenting select 'training pack' handouts on different coloured pieces of paper (soft hues) to help participants locate key pages.
- Get participants more involved in the training by using interactive handouts – see Tam, Leung and Koo (1993) for some useful ideas.
- Never 'read out loud' handouts to participants.
- Give participants sufficient time to read the content of a handout – if you say they have ten minutes make a mental note of the time and give them the full ten minutes (unless they have all finished earlier).
- EIC (2009) suggest offering participants short tasks to complete or questions to answer when reading handouts to aid concentration levels, e.g. list four points X makes about Y; identify two/three key issues in this section; what further questions do you need to ask to understand this section/paragraph/ chapter?
- If you print PowerPoint slides as a handout, use '3 slides per page' to allow space for note taking.
- Think about the value of creating and using e-handouts to save the trees!
- Hole-punch handouts so that they will easily fit into a binder.
- Make sure you proofread handouts to check for clarity, organisation, accuracy, spelling and grammar errors.

Table 7.5 Recommended readings and resources

Source	Title	Author/s	Year	Web link
Practical guide	In plain words: Creating easy-to-read handouts	Cornett, Neal and Ordelt	n.d.	http://tinyurl.com/j6vnmxw
Interactive research paper	Handouts that work: A research based approach to developing teaching handouts	Cox, Churchill and Wellens	2007	http://tinyurl.com/oouxvuq

References

Bligh, D. A. (2000). *What's the Use of Lectures*? San Francisco: Jossey-Bass.

Cornett,S., Neal, W. and Ordelt, K. (n.d.). *In plain words: Creating easy-to-read handouts.* Available at: http://tinyurl.com/j6vnmxw (accessed 22 May, 2017).

Cox, D., Churchill, T. and Wellens, J. (2007). *Handouts that work: A research based approach to developing teaching handouts.* Available at: http://tinyurl.com/oouxvuq (accessed 22 May, 2017).

EIC (2009). *How To Use Handouts Effectively.* Westminster Exchange, University of Winchester. Available at: http://www2.wmin.ac.uk/mcshand/TEACHING/handouts (accessed: 29 June 2017).

Tam, M., Leung, R. W. and Koo, A. (1993). Colloquium: Improving lectures by using interactive handouts. *British Journal of Educational Technology*, 24(2), 139-145.

Wayne State University (n.d.). *How to prepare lecture handouts.* Available at: http://studylib.net/doc/8316430/how-to-prepare-lecture-handouts (accessed 29 June, 2017).

Yoshida, M. (2011). *Creating effective handouts through principals of good design.* Available at: http://tinyurl.com/og56kge (accessed 22 May, 2017).

Chapter 8
Doing

Alan says:

" I often find that getting participants to do something is very often the best assessment. There is a particular practical task that is a requirement of the current GCSE Physics course where students have to change the weight pulling on a trolley and observe how it affects the acceleration of the trolley. It appears to be a really simple practical, but there are quite a few subtleties – in the way that we can differentiate the experiment to suit different ability levels, in how to set up the equipment, and ultimately in how we relate the experiment to the underlying theory. When I am working with teachers I always get them to do the experiment: it instantly highlights any problems they have in understanding the setup and gives a much clearer context when explaining the issues/solutions. 'Doing' the experiment keeps me efficient for the audience I have on the day: it sometimes takes 10 minutes, but can take 35 minutes or longer depending on the group's experience. **"**

Fancy taking part in a quick quiz?

It will only take a minute (promise)!

Imagine a typical training session ...

Q: What do you think is the average attention span of passive participants (in minutes) when the trainer is talking to the whole training group? Please circle just one answer below:

A	B	C	D
8 seconds	7-10 minutes	10-15 minutes	15-20 minutes

Believe it or not, research suggests that it is all of these answers! We recommend that you read the study by Microsoft (2015) to find out about the '8 second attention span shock' (A)! When you think about it, none of the answers above offers a substantial amount of time. This clearly brings the efficacy of traditional training approaches – i.e. the lecture – into question. Hackathorn *et al.* suggest that this commonly used approach 'has developed a reputation of being mundane, disengaging [and] monotonous' (2011: 43). We know only too well (from our personal experiences of being trained by others) that the one-way transmission or 'imparting' of information to participants for long periods of time is an ineffective way of them learning very much from your training. So how can we ensure that participants remain attentive and actually learn something in your training? The answer: by doing!

'Learning by doing'

The notion of 'learning by doing' (Race, 2002) refers to the idea of active learning. Prince suggests that 'active learning is generally defined as any instructional method that engages students in the learning process' (2004: 223). You would be forgiven for thinking that this only applies to children in their formative years; after all, don't little infants learn through play? Yes, and so too can adults! Prominent thinkers such as Bruner (1990) advocate active learning as an approach for all learners, principally because 'all genuine learning is active, not passive. It involves the use of the mind, not just the memory' (Adler, 1982: 23). But this raises an important question: how do we make genuine learning 'active'?

Well, active learning is the process where ... HANG ON! Rather than us just simply telling you, let's get you actively generating some ideas!

Active task

Use the space below to make a written record of different strategies that you have experienced or have observed trainers using to engage participants in active learning as part of their training.

Compare your notes with the remainder of this chapter introduction.

Active learning, by its very name, suggests 'activity', e.g. thinking, talking, making, writing, reflecting, reading, listening and performing. These kinds of activities are purposefully designed to engage participants by including them in the learning process. So why is this important? Well, it relates to the idea of constructivism; a theory of learning 'which emphasises the fact that learners *construct* or *build* their own understanding' (CIE, 2015: 1) and knowledge in response to learning opportunities provided by the trainer. We also see the theory of social constructivism 'in practice' when active learning strategies promote interaction with others, such as the participants' peers. But what ideas actively promote this 'activity' and these theories? Fortunately there is a vast arsenal of strategies available for trainers to choose from, examples of which include:

> problem solving, presentations, group work such as buzz groups, brainstorming, role plays, debates...
> (Revell and Wainwright, 2009: 209)

> teaching, journaling ... focused listening, formulating questions, note taking, annotating...
> (Leibiger, 2015)

> class discussion, small group discussion ... think-pair-share activities, short written exercises and polling the class.
> (Bonwell and Eison, 1991)

Other active learning ideas that complement and validate some of the ideas in the remainder of this chapter include:

- Real-time use of ICT – Encourage participants to use laptops, tablets, smart phones, personal response devices ('clickers') or social media to communicate with trainers to ask questions, respond to questions or give feedback.
- Game play – Engage participants with quick-fire revision games during the training session based on popular television game show formats such as *Jeopardy, Who Wants to Be a Millionaire?* or *Blockbusters*.
- Review writing – Get participants to individually write either a 3-minute 'micro-essay' that summarises the key points of the training session, a list of keywords (between 5 and 7) that define or describe the subject matter that has been learned, or a Review Haiku (adapted from Brownhill, 2015: 82).

It is important to remember that all of these strategies are designed to support the learning experience of participants – there is no point just 'doing' these activities for activities' sake or using them simply to 'fill in' training time. You should therefore think carefully about not just what strategies you intend to use but also why you are using them (remember: aims before activities, see Snapshot B, Planning). Good practice would suggest that this reasoning is verbally shared with participants during the training so that they 'buy in' to the activities offered to them. We know that the true benefits of active learning can only be maximised when:

- The activities offered are authentic and reflect how knowledge and skills are used in real life contexts.
- Learners have opportunities to adopt multiple roles and consider different perspectives.
- Participants are required to articulate their thinking and reflect on the ideas of others.

(adapted from Herrington and Herrington, 2006: 1–13)

By keeping the above in mind, trainers can assure quality 'doing' opportunities that increase the participants' content knowledge, enhance their critical/creative thinking and problem-solving abilities, and build continued positive attitudes towards learning. However, trainers understandably cite a number of difficulties in using active learning strategies in training sessions which hinder them from integrating them into their practice. A selection of these is presented in Table 8.1 with some practical suggestions to positively deal with these difficulties.

In summary:

- Participants learn more in an active learning environment than they do in a passive learning environment.
- Active learning is not simply 'fun and games' – participants will be demonstrating different levels of thinking and 'doing'.
- Actively engaging participants in your training will help them to think more deeply about the training content, bring additional energy to the session, and help you to identify the extent to which they may be finding the material too easy or difficult.

Table 8.1 Practical suggestions to help make the move from lectures to activities (adapted from Brownhill, 2015: 83)

Difficulty	Practical suggestions
"Active learning generates a lot of noise!" (Jack)	▪ Encourage participants to talk quietly to each other before they initiate any discussions/activities. ▪ Signal if participants are talking too loudly with a hand gesture, or by sounding a small hand bell or a digital bleeper.
"Active learning 'eats' into the time needed to cover training content!" (Shamiela)	▪ Get participants to educate each other about training content you cannot fit into the session with reference to specific online materials. ▪ Direct participants to particular readings (electronic, web-based) that build on content that you only give brief mention to in the training session.
"You need a lot of resources and equipment to make training 'active'!" (George)	▪ Assemble an inexpensive resource kit made up of different items such as mini-whiteboards, voting cards (red, green, amber playing-card sized) and sticky notes. Add to this as you think of other useful resources that suit your training style such as an inflatable beach ball or a plastic microphone! ▪ Gradually revise existing training materials with activities that promote dialogue between participants.
"It's too risky! I'm scared that participants won't take part and I will lose control!" (Harriet)	▪ Plan short active learning opportunities (2–3 minutes) to initially build confidence (both participants' and your own). ▪ Establish clear expectations about participants engaging in planned active learning opportunities, emphasising that they will 'only get out what they put in'. ▪ Be positive – trying any new instructional approach will always entail a certain level of risk (but it *will* be worth the risk!).

Table 8.2 Recommended readings and resources

Source	Title	Author/s	Year	Web link
PDF	Active learning and adapting teaching techniques	TATP	n.d.	http://tinyurl.com/ybsppfg7
Article	Active learning strategies in face-to-face courses	Millis	2012	http://tinyurl.com/zx7d4ho
Resource pack*	Active learning and teaching methods for Key Stage 3	Council for the Curriculum, Examinations and Assessment (CCEA)	2007	http://tinyurl.com/nepuvdz

* NOTE! Ideas in this pack can be easily adapted for the adult training context.

Classifying and sorting

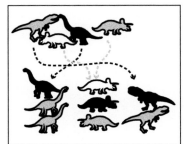

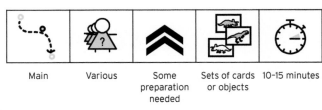

| Main | Various | Some preparation needed | Sets of cards or objects | 10–15 minutes |

A great way of getting participants active, talking and reflecting is by giving them an activity that gets them classifying and sorting (we call this 'organising'). By this we mean putting cards/objects into small groups. The idea is that participants should work together to organise the cards/objects in some way – grouped with similar cards, or rank ordered based on their importance/priority/value/impact etc. Decisions about how the cards/objects might to be organised can be trainer- or participant-led; the same applies to the ways in which the cards/objects are physically arranged, e.g. in a straight line, sets or by building up tiers. Opportunities to justify their choices/decisions can be facilitated by pairing up groups to make critical comparisons.

Benefits
- Ordering and grouping the cards can generate a lot of discussion and in-depth thinking about each of the individual cards, which is probably more important than the final layout.
- Organising materials is recognised as an effective thinking skills tool that has been 'praised for eliciting construct generation and for facilitating talk around a specific topic' (Clark, 2012: 222).

Considerations
- It can take a lot of time to prepare and produce materials for organising (laminating cards assures their durability in the long run). Use and adapt online card sets/object lists where possible to match the focus of your training.

Set-up tips
- Think carefully about where each group is going to organise their materials, e.g. is there enough table space? Could some groups work on the floor/in another room?
- Print individual sets of materials on different coloured card to ensure that sets do not get mixed up when they are in use.

Get individuals to guess what criteria participants from other groups have applied to organise their materials.

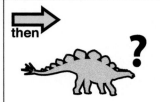

Offer participants an additional card/object for them to integrate into their organised materials – how does this change the layout of the items? Why?

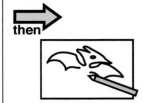

Give participants a blank card for them to add a new item (e.g. a word, a sentence or a sketch of an object) to be organised – why have they added it to the set?

Connect me how?

Prompt participants to keep asking each other 'how' questions during the training to encourage respondents to think about how theories, objects, strategies and ideas on individual pieces of card are connected, e.g. 'How is Bloom's Revised Taxonomy (2001) similar to the original Taxonomy (1956)?' Continue to ask 'how' questions of the answers received to drill down in depth.

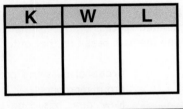

Alternative - Get participants to ask each other 'why' questions to promote critical thought about the 'how' connections, e.g. 'Why were changes made to Bloom's (1956) Taxonomy?'

KWL grid

Invite participants at the start of a session to organise a series of cards based on the subject content of the training for that day using a KWL grid: what we (think we) already **K**now; what we **W**ant to know; what we have **L**earned. As the session progresses, get participants to move cards between the columns as appropriate.

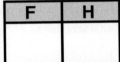

K	W	L

Extension - Suggest participants write new cards for extra columns, such as FH: what **F**urther questions we have; **H**ow we will find out the answers.

F	H

Buy/sell/destroy

Provide participants with a selection of cards on which are presented individual innovative ideas to improve provision and practice. Get them to work together to sort them into those that they would use themselves ('buy'), encourage others to use ('sell') or not use at all ('destroy').

Alternative - Suggest that participants adapt those ideas they would 'destroy' to create a new category, e.g. 'Take it or leave it' or 'Recycle'.

Group discussions and interactions

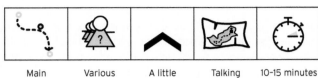

| Main | Various | A little preparation needed | Talking objects (optional) | 10–15 minutes |

Put four participants together and give them a specific task or challenge that they have to solve within ten minutes. For the discussion to be most productive you have to be explicit with the expected outcome of the task. For example, if you were running some training on navigation you might give participants a map with two points along a path marked A and B and they would have to describe what they would see if they walked along the route. After five minutes, circulate around the training room and point out important considerations to any groups that are running out of ideas or are having limited success (in our example it could be to ensure they describe the shape of the land along the path based on the contour lines).

Benefits	■ Group discussions promote co-operation and collaboration between group members.
	■ New ideas based on those proposed by others in the group can be generated within a short period of time.
Considerations	■ Some participants may choose to not take part, may dominate others or may monopolise the group discussion to their advantage; however, this can be minimised if the objectives of the discussion are clear enough and you are emphasising the notion of 'team work'.
	■ Be clear on timings and give frequent reminders.
Set-up tips	■ Think carefully about the size of the groups you want (2s/3–4s/5–7s) and how these might be organised (friendship/colleague/gender/job role).
	■ When you have one minute of time left, circulate around the group again and tell them to finish what they are doing but not to worry about completing the whole activity.

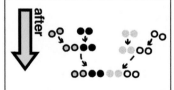

Once pairs of participants have discussed an idea/issue, they can be 'snowballed' together to form a group of 4, then 8, then 16, and then the whole training group to share their thoughts with others.

Invite reporters (those whose role in the group it is to sum up and present ideas) to share their group's thoughts with the rest of the training group 'against the clock'.

Provide time for participants to reflect and converse with others about what they have learned from the discussions of other groups.

Personal case study

Ask one participant to share a problem or issue, which they are hoping that your training will be able to help them with. Their personalised learning aims (see Chapter 1, Pre-course engagement) may help you identify a suitable candidate. Invite other participants to come up with ideas based upon your training, from their own experience or research to help plan a possible 'answer' to try. Ask the original participant how good the 'answer' is, and what other questions or concerns they still have. If you have a group of around 10 or more you may need several smaller groups working on different personal case studies so that every participant remains engaged.

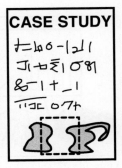

Gallery group discussions

Give small groups a strategy or a theory to critically discuss. Get them to record their conclusions on a piece of flipchart paper ('the gallery') using one pen colour per group before moving to another strategy/theory, recording their conclusions on the easel paper. Once complete, encourage all groups to circulate around the gallery display to see what other groups have added via their coloured contributions.

Alternative - Rather than each group writing down their contributions, invite one participant to stay and commit to memory some of the verbal conclusions drawn by different groups, recalling these as a 'live exhibit' as part of the gallery display.

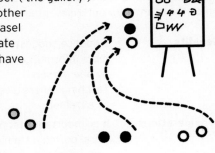

Fishbowl

Organise a group of participants in a small circle (to represent the fishbowl) in the middle of the training room; arrange the rest of the group in a large circle around them. Offer the fishbowl group a topic/question/scenario to discuss, encouraging those in the outer circle to observe, take notes or discuss the thoughts generated by those in the fishbowl with those either side of them.

Alternative - Allow participants in the outer circle to either 'trade places' with those in the fishbowl, thus promoting a kind of a relay-style discussion, or encourage them to periodically 'coach' the fishbowl group from the side lines.

'Educating Alan'

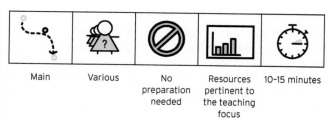

| Main | Various | No preparation needed | Resources pertinent to the teaching focus | 10–15 minutes |

An effective way of getting participants to 'do' and 'learn' at the same time is to invite them to educate others. This is not a new idea; Paul (2011) suggests that people have known this for thousands of years, especially when we reflect on the words of Roman philosopher Seneca: 'While we teach, we learn'. The opportunity to teach others can be achieved by inviting participants to verbalise to others something that they have understood and can remember – this could be in response to a reading, a video, an activity or a discussion. Other suggestions include them devising and sharing a teaching resource (e.g. a presentation or a handout) or leading a practical task from which they can 'draw out' relevant learning.

Benefits	Evidence suggests that teaching others helps participants to remember more information than from training sessions that are delivered or taught by one person.
	Teaching others gives participants an opportunity to practise their skills as a trainer.
Considerations	It is important that participants do not feel as if they are 'doing all of the work' during a training session – use this strategy sparingly, limiting the amount of time participants have to teach, e.g. 10–15 minutes.
	Offer opportunities for participants to either teach individuals (1-2-1), a small group or the whole group depending on their confidence levels and capabilities.
Set-up tips	Ensure that you provide sufficient time as part of your training session for participants to prepare for their teaching opportunity. Have to hand basic teaching resources that they can use if they wish, e.g. pens, paper, scissors, and Blu-tack.

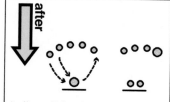

Invite participants to teach not only their peers but also you – challenge them to team-teach with others, educating you in something that you do not already know!

Suggest that participants record their teaching on their smartphone, uploading it onto a shared online repository for other participants to download and learn from.

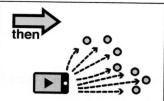

Suggest that participants 'carry on the chain of learning' by using the uploaded videos as part of their own training of colleagues in their place of work.

Working-in-role

Engage participants in some training role play by
assigning them different scenarios that they
could play out in an effort to educate others in
new knowledge, e.g. an educator working hard to
engage reluctant learners, a trainer teaching a film
star in preparation for their new movie role as a
professor, or a small group of students tutoring their
private tutor. Indicate when participants are 'in role'
through character voices, body movements and simple
costumes, e.g. a hat, a coat or a pair of glasses.

Alternative - If you are confident enough, work in role as part of your own training delivery
to gain participant attention and sustain their learning interest (a Simon-favourite strategy!).

Paper knowledge

An interesting way to educate others is through the paper materials that you offer participants.
These are likely to come from a variety of different sources (e.g.
books, journal articles, web resources) – but what about from the
participants themselves? Show them how to make different
paper books (see http://tinyurl.com/hparhc9), giving
them time during your training to collaborate to share
their new knowledge with others through interesting
text and illustrations.

Enrichment - Consider making simple ebooks
using word-processing packages that participants
have easy access to, which they can share with other
participants via email.

Game play

Challenge participants to educate others through making and playing different types of
games. These could be guessing games (e.g. Guess the meaning of the key word/concept;
What word is missing?), simple board games (Classroom
Trivial Pursuit) or dice games (e.g. the digit thrown
matches the number of questions participants can ask
others to test their 'specialist subject
knowledge' – think *Mastermind!*).

Alternative - Signpost participants to
online games that they can play as an
extension to your training to reinforce learning
or serve as a revision exercise in the future.

Making things

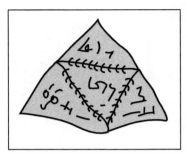

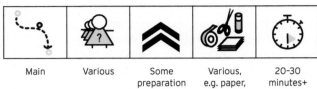

| Main | Various | Some preparation needed | Various, e.g. paper, pens, glue, sticky tape | 20-30 minutes+ |

One way to make your training unmemorable is by too often giving participants large sheets of flipchart paper/pens and asking them to 'make a poster', or asking them to 'create a PowerPoint presentation'. The idea of getting participants to make/create something can be a good one as this helps to practically engage them as part of the training session. However, it is important to offer some variety to what participants make/create whilst getting them to carefully think about why they are making/creating it (it is not there just to fill in time and give you a bit of a rest!). Participants could make 3D models, games (think crossword puzzles, bingo boards and quizzes), Prezi presentations and visual aids/teaching resources to introduce/demonstrate/extend/strengthen learning from the training session.

Benefits
- The emphasis on learning is clearly placed on the part of participants during a training session.
- You have the opportunity to respond to individual needs and formatively assess participants' learning as they 'make things'.

Considerations
- Ensure that the emphasis is placed on the **learning** that comes from the content of the item being made as opposed to the **making** of the item.
- Provide 10/5/2/1 minute warnings (verbal or via visual online timers) to ensure that the time provided for participants to make things does not 'eat' into the rest of the training session.

Set-up tips
- Provide participants with sufficient space to make and create.

Provide opportunities for participants to share their made items with their peers as part of a Learning Showcase.

Invite participants to discuss what they have learned from the items that have been made by others (a useful peer learning opportunity).

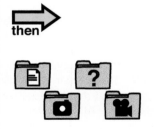

Suggest that participants upload images or scans of the items they have made on a shared online learning space for others to refer to or use as part of their professional role.

Storymaking

The power of story as a learning tool for all ages cannot be underestimated. Invite participants to work together to 'make up a story' to instruct, inform or persuade others to embrace a new theory, utilise a practical learning and teaching strategy, or recognise the importance of new subject knowledge as part of their working role. This story could be written down or performed as a piece of oral storytelling.

Alternative – You could encourage participants to use professional anecdotes from their own working experience to support and entertain others as part of their storymaking.

Learning capsule

Challenge participants to make a learning capsule using a container of their choice (think a cup, a pencil case or a carrier bag) that effectively 'contains' the learning of a small collaborative group in visual form, e.g. sticky notes with keywords on, little sketches, clay models. Rotate the groups around the room and invite them to work out what the learning has been based on the items seen/handled/read/discussed.

Alternative – Suggest that participants take digital images of their learning capsules, sharing them with colleagues back in their workplace as part of a Learning Debrief.

Drill-making

An unusual item for participants to make is a 'learning drill' – 'a session of repetitive practice designed to increase efficiency, improve quality of performance, or aid retention' (see http://tinyurl.com/ourrpck). Ask participants to collaborate with others to devise and lead short learning drills to help peers remember key aspects of what they have read, heard, seen, discussed and undertaken during the training session.

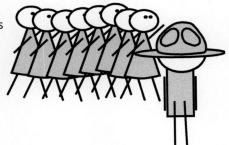

Alternative – Suggest that participants create acronyms, acrostics, rhymes and/or chants to help others remember key aspects of learning from the training session.

References

Adler, M. J. (1982). *The Paideia Proposal: An Educational Manifesto.* New York: Macmillan Publishing Company.

Bonwell, C. and Eison, J. (1991). *Active Learning: Creating Excitement in the Classroom. AEHE-ERIC Higher Education Report No. 1.* Washington, DC: Jossey-Bass.

Brownhill, S. (2015). 'Engaging and educating, not entertaining': Planning for active large lectures. *Pedagogical Dialogue*, 1(11), 80–84.

Bruner, J. S. (1990). *Acts of Meaning.* Cambridge, MA: Harvard University Press.

Cambridge International Examinations (CIE) (2015). *Active learning.* Available at: www.cie.org.uk/images/271174-active-learning.pdf (accessed 9 July, 2016).

Clark, J. (2012). Using diamond ranking as visual cues to engage young people in the research process. *Qualitative Research Journal*, 12(2), 222–237.

Council for the Curriculum, Examinations and Assessment (CCEA) (2007). *Active learning and teaching methods for Key Stage 3.* Belfast: CCEA. Available at: http://tinyurl.com/nepuvdz (accessed 22 May, 2017).

Hackathorn, J., Solomon, E. D., Blankmeyer, K. L., Tennial, R. E. and Garczynski, A. M. (2011). Learning by doing: An empirical study of active teaching techniques. *Journal of Effective Teaching*, 11(2), 40–54.

Herrington, A. and Herrington, J. (2006). What is an authentic learning environment? In: Herrington, A. and Herrington, J. (eds) *Authentic Learning Environments in Higher Education* (pp. 1–13). Hershey, PA: Information Science Publishing.

Leibiger, C. (2015). *Types of active-learning techniques. University of South Dakota.* Available at: http://libguides.usd.edu/content.php?pid=190434&sid=1597402 (accessed 8 July, 2016).

Microsoft (2015). *Attention spans. Consumer insights, Microsoft Canada.* Available at: http://tinyurl.com/qztuo82 (accessed 22 May, 2017).

Millis, B. (2012). *Active learning strategies in face-to-face courses.* Idea Paper 53. Manhatten, KS: The Idea Center. Available at: www.ideaedu.org/Portals/0/Uploads/Documents/IDEA%20Papers/IDEA%20Papers/PaperIDEA_53.pdf (accessed 22 May, 2017).

Paul, A. M. (2011). The protégé effect. *Time*, 30 November. Available at: http://ideas.time.com/2011/11/30/the-protege-effect/ (accessed 18 February, 2016).

Prince, M. (2004). Does active learning work? A review of the research. *Journal of Engineering Education*, 93(3), 223–231.

Race, P. (2002). *The Lecturer's Toolkit: A Practical Guide to Learning, Teaching and Assessment.* London: Kogan Page.

Revell, A. and Wainwright, E. (2009). What makes lectures 'unmissable'? Insights into teaching excellence and active learning. *Journal of Geography in Higher Education*, 33(2), 209–223.

Snapshot H: Motivating adult learners

My name is Michael and I don't want to be here!

Imagine these to be the introductory words of a participant attending your training (unfortunately they were voiced at the start of one of our training sessions!). Even though Dewey (1938) states that the most important attitude that can be formed is a desire to learn, not all training participants are actually motivated to learn, and this can impact on the sessions you deliver and what participants 'take away' from the training. In this Snapshot we briefly consider the factors that serve as barriers to motivation in adult learners, highlighting practical ways to help participants to want to learn during your training.

The Z factor!

There are, as you might expect, numerous reasons as to why adult participants lack motivation to learn (see Table 8.3 for examples):

Table 8.3 Reasons as to why adult participants may lack the motivation to learn

Reason	Research
▪ Age – Older professionals are less likely to willingly take part in adult learning activities than younger ones. ▪ Gender – Men participate less frequently and are less 'inspired' in training than women.	Adapted from Dæhlen and Ure (2009)
▪ A lack of time – Participants may be pressured by mounting professional commitments. ▪ Confidence issues – This is likely to be as a result of their innate disposition. ▪ Interest – The relevance of the training may not match the participant's initial/ continuing professional development needs. ▪ Problems with child care and transportation – Participants may be dealing with numerous personal issues 'outside' of the training.	Adapted from Lieb (1991)
▪ Health issues – Participants could have underlying health problems that affect their outlook and attitudes towards learning. ▪ Geographical location – Participants may have to travel long distances to access the training which outweighs the learning benefits. ▪ Cost – Participants may have had to pay for the training themselves and not consider it 'value for money'.	Adapted from ACE (2008)

We also consider that participants may have a preconceived idea of what the training should be like and what it should cover, and any deviation from this is perceived as a bad thing. Good trainers are not only aware of this multitude of factors but are able to positively address these through a range of practical strategies. So what really works?

Motivate me!

Howard argues that '[i]ncreasing and maintaining learner motivation is a fundamental concern of adult educators' (1989: 205). One way to address this is by recognising and responding to six factors that serve as sources of motivation for adult learning, as suggested by Lieb (1991), shown in Figure 8.1.

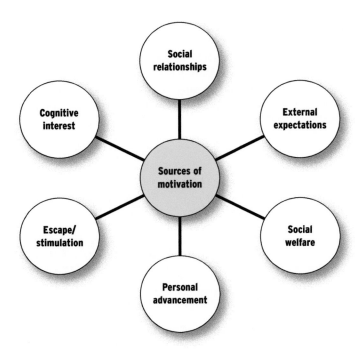

FIGURE 8.1 Six sources of motivation for adult learning (see Lieb, 1991 for more details)

With reference to these six sources and the reasons offered in Table 8.3, we present a 'Choose and Use' strategy scroll (Figure 8.2) that brings together various ways of motivating adult learners that really do work. We have adapted some of the findings of Bixler (2005) to help you further motivate adult learners via a set of quick-fire reminders:

1   Ensure that training materials (think slides, handouts and reading tasks) are appealing, interesting and are presented in a variety of ways.
2   Activities offered should be challenging but not too difficult to accomplish.
3   Integrate participants' prior learning and life experiences into your training input whenever possible.
4   Help participants to recognise the importance of your training by relating it specifically to their learning needs and the training goals.
5   Develop participants' confidence by building a bond with them so they know you will support them in their learning as and when necessary.

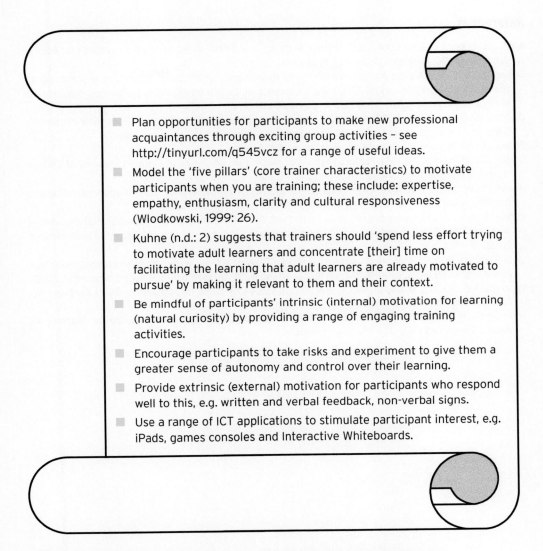

■ Plan opportunities for participants to make new professional acquaintances through exciting group activities – see http://tinyurl.com/q545vcz for a range of useful ideas.

■ Model the 'five pillars' (core trainer characteristics) to motivate participants when you are training; these include: expertise, empathy, enthusiasm, clarity and cultural responsiveness (Wlodkowski, 1999: 26).

■ Kuhne (n.d.: 2) suggests that trainers should 'spend less effort trying to motivate adult learners and concentrate [their] time on facilitating the learning that adult learners are already motivated to pursue' by making it relevant to them and their context.

■ Be mindful of participants' intrinsic (internal) motivation for learning (natural curiosity) by providing a range of engaging training activities.

■ Encourage participants to take risks and experiment to give them a greater sense of autonomy and control over their learning.

■ Provide extrinsic (external) motivation for participants who respond well to this, e.g. written and verbal feedback, non-verbal signs.

■ Use a range of ICT applications to stimulate participant interest, e.g. iPads, games consoles and Interactive Whiteboards.

FIGURE 8.2 'Choose and Use' strategy scroll to help motivate adult learners

Table 8.4 Recommended readings and resources

Source	Title	Author/s	Year	Web link
Guidebook	Innovative Ways for Motivating Adults for Learning	Vacaretu, Kovacs and Steiner (eds)	2011	http://tinyurl.com/jqxn2wv
Academic journal article	Factors that affect motivation among adult learners	Green and Kelso	2006	http://tinyurl.com/pq3yo7f

References

American Council on Education (ACE) (2008). *Mapping new Direction: Higher Education for Older Adults*. Washington, DC: American Council on Education.

Bixler, B. (2005). *Motivation and its relationship to the design of educational games*. Paper presented at the New Media Consortium (NMC) Online Conference on Educational Gaming, December. Available at: www.personal.psu.edu/bxb11/m&g.pdf (accessed 24 December, 2015).

Dæhlen, M. and Ure, O. B. (2009). Low skilled adults in formal continuing education: Does their motivation differ from other learners? *International Journal of Lifelong Education*, 28(5), 661–674.

Dewey, J. (1938). *Experience and Education*. New York: Collier.

Green, T. and Kelso, C. (2006). Factors that affect motivation among adult learners. *Journal of College Teaching and Learning*, 3(4), 65–74.

Howard, K. W. (1989). A comprehensive expectancy motivation model: Implications for adult education and training. *Adult Education Quarterly*, 39(4), 199–210.

Kuhne, G. (n.d.). *10 characteristics of adults as learners*. Available at: http://ctle.hccs.edu/facultyportal/tlp/seminars/tl1071SupportiveResources/Ten_Characteristics_Adults-Learners.pdf (accessed 24 December, 2015).

Lieb, S. (1991). Principles of adult learning. *VISION*, Fall. Available at: www.petsalliance.org/sites/petsalliance.org/files/Lieb%201991%20Adult%20Learning%20Principles.pdf (accessed 2 November, 2016).

Vacaretu, A-S., Kovacs, M. and Steiner, F. (eds) (2011). *Innovative Ways For Motivating Adults For Learning*. Cluj-Napoca, Romania: RWCT IC.

Wlodkowski, R. (1999). *Enhancing Adult Motivation to Learn: A Comprehensive Guide for Teaching All Adults*, Revised edn. San Francisco: Jossey-Bass.

Chapter 9
Independent learning

Simon says:

❝ I struggle with the idea that the training I offer is going to 'give participants everything' – I think it sets me up to fail if they expect to learn everything about the training focus given the pressures on time and resources. That is why I am a real advocate of independent learning – giving participants time and space to learn for themselves. I know that this is difficult if you are only delivering a half-day training session; this is why I like to intersperse Independent Study Tasks (ISTs) throughout my presentations that direct participants to quality readings and tasks to follow up, strengthen or learn about things that I am unable to fit into the training. I know that a good number of participants will not engage in these tasks due to their many work/family commitments, which is why motivating participants to choose and undertake just one of the suggested ISTs is so important. A trainer I know sends an email to all of her participants three weeks after the completion of her training to see how they are getting on and what they learned from the ISTs they have engaged with – I am always surprised by the number of responses that she gets! I like how she always sends them a personal email back in recognition of their efforts and learning – this takes a lot of time but I think this is a great way of keeping participants engaged in independent learning (that's why I am going to try and embrace this as one of my own strategies!). ❞

When the term 'independent learning' is heard or referred to, Knight suggests that many of us think of learners 'going it alone, unaided' (1996: 35). Because of its common usage, the Higher Education Academy warns that this 'pivotal concept' means 'different things to different people, in different disciplines and in different cultures' (2014: 3). Indeed, there is an abundance of 'independent learning' synonyms and interpretations of these terms, many of which you may use or be familiar with (see Table 9.1):

Table 9.1 Popular terms used to describe independent learning (adapted from Kesten, 1987: 9)				
Autonomous learning	Self-directed learning	Student-initiated learning	Teaching for thinking	Self-instruction
Independent study	Project orientation	Discovery and inquiry	Learning to learn	Lifelong learning

However, for the purposes of clarification, we offer Forster's definition of independent learning/study (cited in Candy, 1991: 13):

a process, a method and a philosophy of education: in which a student acquires knowledge by his or her own efforts and develops the ability for inquiry and critical evaluation.

Independent learning is therefore a way of helping participants to learn something for themselves through active investigation and reflection, and has the potential for participants to engage more deeply with the course material. We also believe that independent learning is not simply 'learning on your own'. This has important implications for your thinking and the way that you work with participants, the most prominent of which is that you should remember that you are not the only influencing factor in helping participants to learn; participants are able to learn for themselves and from others if they are given opportunities to do this during training sessions.

This shift of responsibility from the trainer to the participant in relation to the learning process means that at times you will be more of a facilitator of learning than an imparter of knowledge. There is a danger that this change in role may be perceived as a way of making the trainer role redundant, but this is far from the case: you need to think carefully about how you can enable and support independent learning as part of the training that you offer. This can be 'fostered by creating opportunities and experiences that encourage learner motivation, curiosity, self-confidence and self-reliance' (Meyer *et al.*, 2008: 15). But what does this look like in practice? To help us answer this question we turn to the work of Cheminais (2015) who highlights a number of internal skills that influence successful independent learning. These skills are important as they can help to maximise the potential for learning from those independent opportunities that you offer participants. We also draw on the work of Edgbaston High School for Girls (2012: 3), adapting their summary in an effort to highlight what these skills are, what is involved, and what the implications for practice are (see Table 9.2):

Table 9.2 Internal skills that influence successful independent learning and associated implications for practice

Examples	What is involved	Implications for practice
Cognitive skills	This refers to the participant's mental ability. It includes them recognising how they think and learn, how they can improve their memory and their attention, embracing effective ways of acquiring and understanding information, and using different strategies to solve problems.	Plan opportunities for participants to: ▪ construct informal rules for solving problems ▪ classify objects according to given/ self-formulated criteria ▪ form hypotheses ▪ reason logically.
Meta-cognitive skills	This refers to the participant's ability to reflect on and assess their own thinking. It involves them reflecting on their strengths and weaknesses generally and within a particular task, as well as thinking about how this can be improved.	Plan opportunities for participants to: ▪ describe how they learn ▪ identify key activities essential for their learning ▪ reflect on what they have done and learned ▪ monitor their progress ▪ use self-assessment so that they can take responsibility for their own learning.
Affective skills	This refers to the participant's feelings and emotions that motivate them to learn despite the difficulties that they may encounter. The most important affective skills include: self-motivation, persistence, seeing themselves as a competent learner, and understanding that a person's attitude can affect their ability to succeed and learn.	Plan opportunities for participants to: ▪ express and manage their own feelings ▪ feel motivated to want to learn independently ▪ wait for achievement outcomes (referred to as the 'delay of gratification').

Cheminais (2015) also presents two external factors that influence successful independent learning. The 'relationship between participants and trainers' (adapted) is important as you are encouraged to move towards a more process-orientated style of training as this helps participants to see that they already have a wealth of experience to build upon. We explore the second external factor – 'an enabling physical environment' – in Figure 9.1 with reference to MacBeath's (1993: 9) hierarchy of environmental support, which he argues is needed for independent learning, considering what you need to think about.

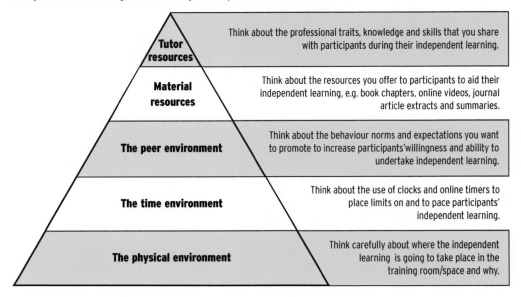

FIGURE 9.1 MacBeath's (1993) hierarchy of environmental support for independent learning (adapted)

So what ideas can help you to put independent learning into practice? We offer you the table below (Table 9.3) in an effort to promote some 'reader-choice' of the practical ideas you might want to independently learn about for the benefit of your training provision.

Table 9.3 Practical ideas for encouraging independent learning and thinking (adapted from DeLong, 2009: 8)

Practical ideas for encouraging independent learning and thinking			Author(s)
Utilising collaborative instructional techniques:			
Divergent thinking	Concept mapping	Journal writing	Saskatchewan Education (n.d.)
Learning centres	Inquiry process	Independent research	
Research-feedback-reflection	Distance education	Virtual field trip	Briggs *et al.* (2007)
Active learning activities:			
Visual-based instruction	In-class writing	Case studies	Bonwell and Eison (1991)
Cooperative learning	Debates	Drama	
Role-playing	Simulation	Peer teaching	
Interactive lectures	Project work	Seminars	Chhem (2000)
Problem-based learning	Small-group discussions		

Table 9.4 succinctly summarises what independent learning is and is not, and serves as a useful reference point when you think about the place and purpose of independent learning opportunities in your training.

TABLE 9.4 What independent learning *is* and *is not* (adapted from Gill and Halim, 2007: 5)

Independent learning is...	Independent learning is NOT...
about designing a variety of participant-centred activities or tasks	leaving participants without any guidance or supervision
empowering participants to use their own strategies and resources	about having less training session preparation to do
about clarifying learning objectives, task requirements and expectations, and checking in at different junctures	about the trainer having more time for himself or herself.
an opportunity to work with individuals whilst the rest of the group remains productive	
believing that participants are capable and resourceful	
about motivating and developing participants to be more confident.	

Table 9.5 Recommended readings and resources

Source	Title	Author/s	Year	Web link
Paper	Teaching methods to encourage independent learning and thinking	DeLong	2009	http://tinyurl.com/y9mg43mj
Academic journal	Guided independent learning: a teaching and learning approach for adult learners	Hsu, Hamilton and Wang	2015	http://tinyurl.com/pfmqv3b
Thesis	Independent adult learning	Brookfield	1980	http://tinyurl.com/zf2b742

Research and read

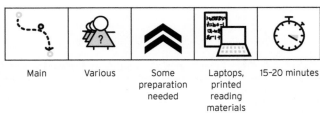

| Main | Various | Some preparation needed | Laptops, printed reading materials | 15-20 minutes |

Encourage participants to use their laptops, tablets or smart-phones to engage in 'desk research', exploring online sources (websites, videos and open access academic papers) to follow up ideas you have introduced them to as part of your training input. Alternatively, you could present participants with a selection of printed materials (think magazine articles, newspaper cuttings, professional journal articles and book extracts) for them to investigate that may be linked to a key theme or concept.

Benefits
- Opportunities like this put the onus for learning back on the participant rather than the emphasis being always on the trainer teaching them.
- Encouraging participants to research what they want to learn about can be very motivating.

Considerations
- Offer some direction for those participants who may not have a clear focus for their research by offering verbal suggestions or displaying ideas.
- Display visible timers so that participants can maximise the research time they have available to them.
- Suggest that participants first 'skim and scan' (see Chapter 7, Engaging with texts) the information they access, reading small samples or extracts rather than trying to digest the whole text.

Set-up tips
- Make sure that any links or materials you provide have high-quality content, and are easy to read/navigate.
- When preparing printed materials, make several copies of each item to allow more than one participant to read it at the same time.

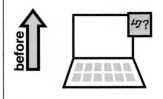

Give participants three minutes to write on a sticky note some questions that they need answering; stick these on the outside of their computer monitor so their focus is clear to both you and them.

Maintain the independent learning theme by asking participants to then plan what they are going to do to remember or implement the results of their research.

Encourage participants to verbally share what they have researched with others in an effort to strengthen their learning, during their coffee break or as a support network after the training.

Real research

Get participants to independently conduct short interviews (5–10 minutes) with individuals from the training group, or external professionals with more experience. Participants should ask questions that relate to the training focus and practices associated with this in their professional setting. Invite participants to reflect on the data they collect, considering its value to their personal learning.

Alternative – Allow participants to write and ask their own interview questions so that they can gather data that is specific to their area/aspect of professional interest.

Converting research

Provide participants with pens and paper that they can use to convert text-based information they have researched into a more accessible format, e.g. turning a new teaching procedure into a set of simple cookery-style instructions, or translating a theory into a diagram, flowchart or sketch.

Extension – Challenge individuals to convert generated pictures, models or charts back into a piece of 'researched text' to see if participants have fully understood the ideas being depicted.

Reciprocal research

Work with one participant, helping them to research a particular idea, model or strategy. Encourage them to then work with a peer in the group, supporting the new person to research the same idea, model or strategy by exploring the same or different materials. Repeat this process several times for the benefit of those who struggle with individual independent learning opportunities.

Alternative – Welcome participants in supporting you to research a particular concept, theory or suggestion that they have investigated. How about reporting back to the whole training group to check your understanding?!

Case studies

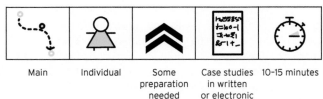

| Main | Individual | Some preparation needed | Case studies in written or electronic format | 10–15 minutes |

Offer participants the chance to learn for themselves about key concepts, ideas or strategies 'in context' during the training session. Provide them with case studies that are based on personal/professional experiences or are taken/adapted from professional readings, media/inspection reports, policies or research findings. Give participants time to individually read and reflect on the narrative provided, encouraging them to draw comparisons to their own personal/professional context. Facilitate time and space for participants to share with their peers their thoughts about the case study in an effort to stimulate discussion and critical thought, encouraging this through the presentation of a range of reflective questions.

Benefits
- Case studies shift the emphasis from trainer-centred activity to more participant-centred activity during a training session.
- Case studies help to bridge the gap between theory and practice by applying theoretical concepts to a recognisable context.

Considerations
- Participants are more likely to see the relevance of case studies if there is a 'link' to their professional context.
- Use pseudonyms to protect the identity of professionals if the case studies you offer are based on real events.

Set-up tips
- Tailor case studies to the context and interests of participants with reference to information gleaned from their pre-course engagement (see Chapter 1). Prepare and display questions prior to participants engaging with the case study so that they know what they are to reflect on.

before 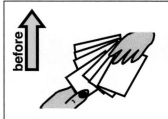	after 	then **Writing text** Edit
Offer participants a range of relevant case studies for them to select from so that they compare and contrast them.	Present individual case studies in the middle of a large sheet of paper (A3) for participants to record their thoughts and ideas in written form around the outside.	Get participants to rewrite parts of the case study to reflect the practice that they have/would use in their own professional role.

Opener and closer

Present case studies to participants as either a starter (at the start of a training session) to introduce a new concept to them or as a plenary (at the end of the training session) to allow participants to apply and synthesise the concepts discussed. Provide opportunities for participants to discuss these by 'drawing out the learning' in response to a series of suggested 'probing prompts'.

Alternative – Invite participants to verbally share case studies of success based on their own professional experiences in relation to the focus of the training session, promoting active listening skills in other participants (see http://tinyurl.com/jcn66yo).

Video case studies

Prepare a video case study to show participants during the training session; this could be a face-to-camera interview, a YouTube video or an excerpt from a previously televised programme (check copyright issues relating to this). Invite participants to make a written record of their thoughts and questions as they watch the video. Organise them into small groups so that they can 'pool' their ideas together with purposeful dialogue.

Alternative – Prepare and play a case study in the form of a voice recording captured on a dictaphone or on tape for reflection and review purposes.

A, B or C case studies

Provide participants with a written description (just one or two sentences) of an open-ended incident or a situation that relates to the focus of the training session. Offer participants a small number of different choices (A, B or C) that serve as possible solutions for them to discuss and debate with other participants in the training room. Ensure that the choices/solutions provide different interpretations and ways in which the incident or situation could be managed or addressed effectively.

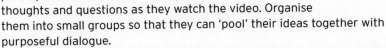

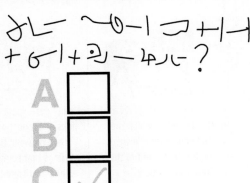

Alternative – Encourage participants to role play the incident or situation to build confidence skills and develop creative problem-solving capabilities, especially if they have to come up with the 'A, B or C' options themselves.

'Own' what you read!

| Main | Individual, group, whole group | Some preparation needed | Reading materials (various) | 15–20 minutes |

Many trainers give participants opportunities to independently engage with reading materials as part of a training session. Encourage participants to 'own' the materials they are reading – this can be achieved by getting them to add new information and ideas to the text, delete points that participants do not feel are important, 'tweak' sentences for cohesion purposes or reorganise the information to help readers digest the material more easily. By doing this, trainers can monitor what participants are learning from their 'owned' materials by asking questions and engaging them in individual critical discussion.

Benefits
  ■ 'Owning' materials encourages participants to read with more depth of understanding rather than at a surface level, i.e. basic levels of comprehension.

Considerations
  ■ Some participants may find it easier to work with others when asked to 'own' materials they read/engage with – offer this as a supportive way to promote cooperation and critical thinking between participants.

Set-up tips
  ■ Gather together a bank of materials in both paper and electronic formats so that participants have a choice as to how they would like to access the material.
  ■ Ensure that there are scissors, glue and coloured paper for those participants who want to 'edit' paper-based materials; encourage those who prefer to 'own' electronic materials to use laptops/tablets etc.

Pair up participants to do a 'Two-Minute-Sell' in which they each summarise their 'owned' reading for the benefit of the other participant.

Invite participants to identify any links or connections which can be made between the two 'owned' readings that support, challenge or extend participants' new learning.

Ask participants to email 'owned' materials to a central online depository for other participants to access and discuss after the training session; electronic documents and scanned copies are equally welcome.

Ask and answer a question

Invite participants to write/verbalise a question or
two about their reading materials before they actively
engage with it. Once read, get participants to see if
they are able to answer their question(s) or not.

Extension - For participants who are unable to
answer their question/s, get them to talk to others to see
if other materials offer the answers that they were looking for.

Peer ownership

Get participants who have engaged with the same
reading material to come together and engage in
some peer-ownership assessment, asking each other
questions to ascertain whether participants took the
same points from the reading or different things.

Alternative - Bring in a third participant to act as a
quiz master, asking each participant some questions to
identify similarities and differences in their responses
and understanding.

All for one and one for all

Generate questions that participants would like to explore
in response to one reading given to each person in the
whole group. Get small groups to read relevant parts of
the material in response to a designated question,
feeding back orally or in written form to the rest of
the group.

Alternative - Use different types of questions from
Wallace's (2000) 'Thinking Wheel' to offer a different focus
for one reading given to the whole group.

References

Bonwell, C. C. and Eison, J. A. (1991). Active learning: Creating excitement in the classroom. *ERIC Digest*, September. Available at: www.ericdigests.org/1992-4/active.htm (accessed 5 December, 2015).

Briggs, L. E., Marks, P. and Skidmore, J. M. (2007). *Introducing the Undergraduate Learner to Independent Learning through Targeted Transferable Skills Acquisition.* ELI Annual Meeting 2007, 24 January.

Brookfield, S. (1980). *Independent adult learning.* PhD thesis, University of Leicester. Available at: http://tinyurl.com/zf2b742 (accessed 22 May, 2017).

Candy, P. (1991). *Self-Direction for Lifelong Learning: A Comprehensive Guide to Theory and Practice.* San Francisco: Jossey-Bass.

Cheminais, R. (2015). *Special Educational Needs for Qualified and Trainee Teachers: A Practical Guide to the New Changes,* 3rd edn. London: David Fulton.

Chhem, R. K. (2000). Spoon-feeding in higher education. *CDTL Brief,* 3(2), 6. Available at: www.cdtl.nus.edu.sg/brief/Pdf/v3n2.pdf (accessed 5 December, 2015).

DeLong, S. (2009). *Teaching methods to encourage independent learning and thinking.* Unpublished paper. Available at: www.usma.edu/cfe/Literature/DeLongS_09.pdf (accessed 5 December, 2015).

Edgbaston High School for Girls (2012). *Independent learning.* Available at: www.edgbastonhigh.co.uk/assets/docs/IndependentLearning-May12.pdf (accessed 5 December, 2015).

Gill, G. K. and Halim, N. A. (2007). *The "I" in independent learning: The rise of self-managing learners.* Paper presented at the Australian Association for Research in Education Conference 'Research Impacts: Proving or Improving', Fremantle. Available at: www.aare.edu.au/data/publications/2007/gil07012.pdf (accessed 5 December, 2015).

Higher Education Academy (HEA) (2014). *Independent learning.* Available at: www.heacademy.ac.uk/system/files/resources/independent_learning.pdf (accessed 5 December, 2015).

Hsu, J., Hamilton, K. and Wang, J. (2015). Guided independent learning: a teaching and learning approach for adult learners. *International Journal of Innovation and Learning,* 17(1), 111–113.

Kesten, C. (1987). *Independent learning: a common essential learning.* A study completed for the Saskatchewan Department of Education Core Curriculum Investigation Project. Saskatchewan Department of Education, University of Regina.

Knight. P. (1996). Independent study, independent studies and 'core skills' in higher education. In: Tait, J. and Knight. P. (eds) *The Management of Independent Learning* (pp. 29–37). London: Kogan Page in association with SEDA.

MacBeath, J. (1993). *Learning for yourself: Supported study in Strathclyde schools.* Strathclyde: Strathclyde Regional Council. Available at: http://files.eric.ed.gov/fulltext/ED362259.pdf (accessed 5 December, 2015).

Meyer, B., Haywood, N., Sachdev, D. and Faraday, S. (2008). *Independent learning: Literature review.* (Research Report: DCSF-RR051). Nottingham: Department for Children, Schools and Families. Available at: www.curee.co.uk/files/publication/[site-timestamp]/Whatisindependentlearningandwhatarethebenefits.pdf (accessed 21 April, 2017).

Saskatchewan Education (n.d.). *Understanding the Common Essential Learnings: A Handbook for Teachers.* Available at: http://publications.gov.sk.ca/documents/11/15377-Understanding-CEL.pdf (accessed 7 September, 2017).

Wallace, B. (2000). *Teaching the Very Able Child: Developing a Policy and Adopting Strategies for Provision.* London: David Fulton.

Snapshot I: Inclusive training

For many years the Institute of Physics has been working on improving the gender balance in physics. It has carried out significant research to figure out how this can be improved in the school context; this has been reported in publications such as 'Opening doors: A guide to good practice in countering gender stereotyping in schools' (IOP, 2015). Many of the results of its research are applicable to any subject and are designed to improve equality for all; the Institute of Physics has also produced an excellent '10 tips for teachers' summary document (IOP, 2016). Exemplification of these principles should be identifiable in many of the training ideas we have offered you within this book.

Most of their conclusions also apply equally well to any adult training context and should be embedded into high-quality training. So, with the Institute of Physics' permission, we include a summary here, adapted for adult trainees.

- Use everyday language – Women (and men) can be intimidated by technical jargon. Avoid it unless it is necessary.
- Allow time for paired or group discussions – Give time for participants to discuss answers to challenging questions before asking them to share ideas with the group.
- Avoid asking for volunteers – Men may be more likely to raise their hands, call out answers and volunteer to take part in demonstrations/activities. Other techniques, such as individual whiteboards or selecting participants at random, can broaden the ways in which people can participate.
- Challenge discriminatory language – Treat sexist language as being just as unacceptable as racist and homophobic language.
- Assign roles for practical work – Men often dominate practical work while women will sometimes hang back and perform written tasks. To avoid this, you can assign roles or use single-sex groups when there are practical elements to your training.
- Monitor your interactions with women and men – You might be surprised at the ratio of men to women who ask or answer questions in your training. Keep a note yourself or ask a colleague to observe one of your sessions to keep count.
- Use gender-neutral contexts whenever possible – Try to avoid using examples that focus on stereotypically male or female hobbies or interests.

Table 9.6 Recommended readings and resources

Source	Title	Author/s	Year	Web link
Website and research-based information	Gender balance	IOP	2016	http://tinyurl.com/g1rl135

References

Institute of Physics (IOP) (2015). *Opening doors: A guide to good practice in countering gender stereotyping in schools*. Available at: www.iop.org/publications/iop/2015/file_66429.pdf (accessed 1 November, 2016).
Institute of Physics (IOP) (2016). *10 inclusive science teaching tips for teachers*. Available at: www.talk physics.org/wp-content/uploads/2016/09/Top-ten-tips-poster.pdf (accessed 13 November, 2016).

Learning phase 4

Monitoring, evaluating and planning for the future

Chapter 10
Providing feedback

Simon says:

"	I think it is so true: everyone wants to know how they are doing. When working with adults I have found that they want to know more about what they are doing wrong and how to address this rather than be told what they are doing well – for children it seems to be the direct opposite! Providing feedback can be time-consuming but there is no doubt in my mind that it can be a valuable way of communicating with participants, particularly if there are 40 people attending your week's training course and you are offering them individual written formative feedback on a piece of work for their portfolio. Immediate feedback is definitely the best, be it in a one-to-one, in a small group situation or as a whole training group – that is why I am ever mindful of the levels of feedback I am giving during a training session. Some may sneer at the use of sticky stars as a way of feeding back to participants but I have found adults really respond to these when they are given as a visual measure of the effort they are putting in (Alan is particularly fond of these!). I have also found that peer feedback only truly works when participants have clear success criteria and that they understand this; without it the feedback is pretty worthless. **"**

Imagine you are a contestant on a 'cheesy' new quiz show called *Tremendous Training!* You have successfully answered all of the starter questions about how to establish participants' existing knowledge, and have breezed your way through the different rounds on Talk, Doing and Independent learning (weren't you glad you read those chapters in this book before you went on the show?!). Now you come to the 'Killer Questions'. Answer them all correctly and you win today's mystery star prize (*'Oooooooooo!'*). The first question is:

'What do participants actually need from your training?'

You pause to think ...

How would you answer this 'Killer Question'?

Interestingly, Sockalingam (2012) sought the views of over 2000 students at a Singapore university in an effort to try to understand what adult learners needed from their instructors. One of the seven categories that emerged from the data related to the notion of constructive feedback. This chapter introduction explores this 'critical component' of good training, considering what is meant by feedback, the place and purpose of feedback as part of the learning process, the different types of feedback you can offer participants, and ways in which this can be provided. We structure this chapter introduction by using some questions taken from other episodes of *Tremendous Training!*

So, contestant number one, we start with you and it's a multiple-choice question. The question is: What is feedback? Is it:

A. 'a constructive and objective appraisal of performance' (Katz, 2006: 2)

B. 'any communication or procedure given to inform a learner of the accuracy of a response, usually to an instructional question' (Mory, 2004: 745), or

C. 'all dialogue to support learning in both formal and informal situations' (Askew and Lodge, 2000: 1)?

Unsurprisingly, given the references offered at the end of each definition, feedback can be A, B and C!. Despite there being no definitive definition of the term, it is important that you are clear about the different categories or 'purposes' of feedback that exist as these will shape the kinds of feedback that you can give to participants during your training. We offer these in the form of a 'nested hierarchy' of roles (from basic correction to feed-forward) that we have adapted from the work of Price *et al.* (2010: 278–9) (see Table 10.1).

Table 10.1 The hierarchy of types of feedback

Role	Meaning	Example
5. Longitudinal development (feed-forward)	Supporting improvements for future work	"Next time think about A, B and C"
4. Benchmarking	Identifying a gap between what is understood/has been demonstrated and the standard of performance expected	"You know about X but your lack of understanding about Y affects your ability to reflect on Z"
3. Forensic diagnosis	Diagnosing problems with the work	"You seem to just *describe* events rather than *reflect critically* on them"
2. Reinforcement	Providing positive or negative reinforcement to behaviour	"Have a sticky star for your excellent effort in this session"
1. Correction	'Putting things right' by taking a corrective action	"You need to change the spelling of 'Scinnur' to 'Skinner'"

Hello there, contestant number two. Your question is: What is the place and purpose of feedback as part of the learning process?

Those who subscribe to the constructivist paradigm believe that learners construct their own meaning and knowledge by actively engaging in the learning process. This is developed by Vygotsky (1978) who claims that our construction of knowledge can be expanded and improved under the guidance of capable adults (i.e. you as a trainer) or peers. Feedback should be ultimately designed to help participants develop as a professional. In order to ensure that this happens, Hattie and Timperley (2007: 86) assert that 'the main purpose of feedback is to reduce discrepancies between current understandings and performance and a goal'. With this in mind, you are recommended to focus your feedback, 'addressing fundamental feedback questions including "where am I going", "how am I going", and "where to next"' (Hattie, 2011:

2). This can be achieved by giving feedback that relates specifically to the success criteria set for the task ('where am I going'), the progress that participants have made in relation to a specific part of the task ('how am I going') and helping them to target areas for development ('where to next').

We now move to contestant number three. Are you ready for your question? The question on the card is: What different types of feedback can you offer participants?

The two broad categories of feedback you are likely to be aware of are positive and negative. Put simply, positive feedback focusses on 'the good' or the strengths in a participant's performance, whilst negative feedback identifies 'the bad' or areas/aspects that are in need of development. We all like receiving positive feedback, and to keep participants motivated in our training we think that it is a good idea to share with them what they are doing well. However, this needs to be 'balanced up' with suggestions as to what they can improve to constructively help participants to keep developing, both personally and professionally (remember: no one is perfect, except possibly Kylie Minogue).

Keyton (2005: 271-2) presents three types of feedback that we find particularly useful:

- Descriptive feedback – This merely identifies or describes what is seen/read/heard.
- Evaluative feedback – This goes beyond mere description and provides an evaluation or assessment of the task/observation/work produced.
- Prescriptive feedback – This provides participants with advice about how they should work/practise/write.

We recommend, however, that you remain mindful of the two broad categories of feedback as previously discussed (positive and negative) as these can help you to 'shape' the feedback you give, e.g. descriptive feedback that targets the negatives or evaluative feedback that recognises the positives.

NOTE!
Ideas presented in this chapter focus more on the different ways in which these types of feedback can be communicated to participants, e.g. through oral (verbal) and written means.

Contestant number four! Thanks for your patience! Your question is: In what ways can feedback be provided to participants?

Race (2001) offers a valuable suite of strategies that trainers can select from and adapt (as we have done in Table 10.2) to feedback to participants. We recommend that you take a look at Race's work (a suggested Recommended reading in Table 10.3) as he presents a balanced set of advantages and disadvantages for each of the strategies presented in Table 10.2, thus allowing you to make an informed choice about strategies you would like to include in your training toolkit.

Table 10.2 Strategies for providing feedback to course participants

---

Feedback in writing or print

- ☐ Handwritten comments on (or about) participants' assessed work.
- ☐ Word-processed overall comments on each participant's assessed work.
- ☐ Model answers or solutions that are issued to participants along with their assessed work.
- ☐ Assignment feedback return sheets.
- ☐ Word-processed overall cohort reports on an assigned piece of work.
- ☐ Codes written on participants' work that are debriefed in a whole-group session.

Face-to-face feedback

- ☐ To individual participants.
- ☐ To small groups of participants.
- ☐ To the whole cohort.

Electronic feedback

- ☐ Emailed comments on participants' assessed work.
- ☐ Using computer conferences for overall comments on batches of participants' work.
- ☐ Computer-delivered feedback – '(pre-prepared) feedback responses to structured self-assessment questions in computer-based learning packages' (Race 2001: 10).

Given the advances in technology over the last 15+ years, we recognise that participants can also receive feedback via other electronic methods such as text messages, social media platforms, virtual learning environments, video conferencing and blogs.

Irrespective of which strategies you ultimately decide to use, it is important that the feedback you give, be it informal or formal, emulates certain characteristics, e.g. it is:

- ☐ 'clear ... specific ... encouraging' (Shrivastava *et al.*, 2014); and
- ☐ 'objective, consistent, and timely' (Sachdeva, 1996: 106).

In summary:

- ☐ Despite there being no definitive definition of the term 'feedback', there are a number of roles attributed to its main purpose. These include correction, reinforcement and benchmarking.
- ☐ Good feedback addresses the 'fundamental feedback questions' as proposed by Hattie (2011), which include 'where am I going', 'how am I going' and 'where to next'?
- ☐ There are different types of feedback and ways in which this feedback can be given to participants. These include descriptive, evaluative and prescriptive feedback. Ways to give this to participants can be in written or verbal form.
- ☐ Good feedback emulates certain characteristics that trainers should be mindful of, e.g. clear, specific, encouraging and consistent.

Table 10.3 Recommended readings and resources

Source	Title	Author/s	Year	Web link
PDF document	Using feedback to help students to learn	Race	2001	http://tinyurl.com/lotuuru
Web page	20 ways to provide effective feedback for learning	Reynolds	2013	http://tinyurl.com/j37jr28
Word document	The art of giving and receiving feedback	Mehay	n.d.	http://tinyurl.com/ks9p8qb

---

Providing written feedback

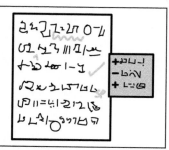

Post-session	Individual	Lots of preparation needed	Feedback proforma (optional)	5-15 minutes

Participants who complete written work as part of your training (think learning logs, reflective accounts and short essays) are likely to expect written feedback from you. This is typically given at the end of a training day/week when you have time to mark the work that has been submitted. The 'Feedback Sandwich' is a useful 3-point strategy that helps you to consistently make a summative positive statement, highlight an area for improvement and then finish with another positive statement. If participants are drafting pieces of work during your training sessions, you might offer formative written feedback on a sample/extract using a simple key, e.g. <✓>= accurate reference, <^>= missing word, <~~>= unclear meaning, and <SP> = spelling error. In both cases this written feedback can be handwritten or given in an electronic format.

Benefits	■ Most participants actively want this kind of feedback from you!
	■ Written feedback 'provides an enduring record and reference point that [participants] can take away and reflect on at a later date' (University of Westminster, n.d.: 8).
Considerations	■ Be clear, concise and constructive.
	■ You can save time by creating feedback proformas or grids that allow you to tick figures on a scale of achievement. It can be helpful to share this whilst participants are writing.
Set-up tips	■ Be clear about what aspect you are to give written feedback on for consistency purposes, e.g. the learning goals (their demonstration of subject knowledge) or performance goals (their writing tone).

Invite participants to look at a section of their work whilst keeping your formative feedback in mind from a previous section you have commented on: 'How could you use this to develop this section?'

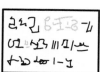

Ask participants to indicate how they have amended their work in response to your formative written feedback, e.g. with different coloured text, highlighters or annotations.

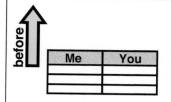

Encourage participants to self-assess their work before giving them their written summative feedback. Use the same proforma to record this self-assessment/summative feedback.

Stop/start/continue

When offering written feedback to participants, structure it so that it explains what you feel they should **stop** doing in their work, what you feel they should **start** doing in their work, and what you hope they will **continue** doing.

Alternative - Use the 'Plus, minus and what's next?' approach to give written feedback to participants, linking written comments to plus/minus signs and question marks around their work.

Feedback/feedforwards

Give participants written feedback that not only reflects on what they have done well and what they could improve on (feedback), but also explains how they could make improvements to their subsequent work (feed-forwards), e.g. 'Next time think about ...'

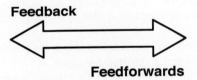

Feedback

Feedforwards

Extension - Before participants start a new piece of work give them time to look back at the improvement suggestions you previously made so that they can positively 'act on' these.

Exemplars

Provide participants with exemplar pieces of work (fictional/actual; varying quality) that include both formative and summative written feedback. Invite participants to consider how this feedback might apply to their own work.

Alternative - Suggest that participants write their own formative and summative feedback on 'blank' exemplar pieces of work to promote critical discussion and thinking.

Providing oral feedback

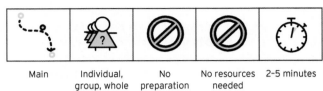

| Main | Individual, group, whole group | No preparation needed | No resources needed | 2-5 minutes |

Oral feedback is the most regular and interactive form of feedback you can use in your training. Ask participants open-ended questions (e.g. 'Why do you think this strategy will not work?') or engage them in a dialogue (e.g. 'Tell me about how you would deal with this situation') so that you can 'find out what [participants] already know, identify gaps in [their] knowledge and understanding, and scaffold the development of their understanding' (Brighton and Hove City Council Hub, 2016). In response to this, offer participants verbal feedback that not only acknowledges 'strength' in their responses (think clarity of explanation, depth of understanding or level of reflection) but also helps them to think about ways of developing their thinking/work (consider alternative points of view, revisiting a theory or adapting a new idea).

Benefits
- Oral feedback has been found to have a greater impact on participants' work/thinking than written feedback.
- You can offer oral feedback to participants who are engaged in independent learning activities, working collaboratively in small groups and as a whole group.

Considerations
- Oral feedback is transient – it is not easy for some participants to reflect accurately on this type of feedback as they are likely to only remember particular parts of it.

Set-up tips
- Be mindful of the most appropriate ways of offering oral feedback – general oral feedback is best delivered to groups (public); save specific personalised oral feedback for individuals (private).
- Consider your tone of voice, facial expressions and body language – there is more to giving oral feedback than just spoken words!

Give participants time to absorb the oral feedback you offer them, responding to this (if possible/appropriate) within the timeframe of the training session.

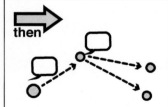

Invite participants to orally share the oral feedback they have received from you with others to benefit their work/thinking.

Follow up your oral feedback later on in the training session with visual cues, e.g. a 'thumbs up', a smile or an OK hand gesture, or written feedback.

Hear it/see it/share it/learn from it!

Invite participants to digitally record the oral feedback you give (think smartphones, dictaphones). Suggest that they transcribe individual points onto sticky notes (speech bubble shaped), which are then attached to their 'work-in-progress' for others to read, reflect on and learn from.

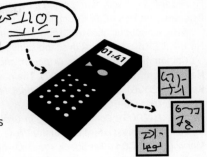

Extension - Get participants to record the oral responses that other participants make in response to your written oral feedback, responding positively to this via revisions to their work.

Three guesses

Challenge participants to predict the content of the oral feedback that you will give them. Structure their thinking by encouraging them to consider: (a) what they think they have done well, (b) what needs improvement, and (c) how they could improve it. How do their predictions compare to your actual oral feedback?

Alternative - Invite participants from other groups to act as the 'trainer', getting participants to predict their oral feedback (how does this compare to what you were going to say?).

In-session conferencing

When working with participants over a 1-2 week training period, consider planning individual meetings with participants during training sessions where you can orally feedback to them, focussing on their progress and targets whilst the rest of the group engage in independent learning activities.

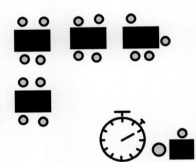

Alternative - If participants require more time than you can give them during a training session, conduct an out-of-session conference either before or after the training day.

References

Askew, S. and Lodge, C. (2000). Gifts, ping-pong and loops-linking feedback and learning. In: Askew, S. (ed.) *Feedback for Learning* (pp. 1–17). London: Routledge.

Brighton and Hove City Council Hub (2016). *Focus – effective assessment – oral feedback*. Available at: www.school-portal.co.uk/GroupHomepage.asp?GroupId=1194688 (accessed 18 June, 2016).

Hattie, J. (2011). Feedback in schools. In: Sutton, R., Hornsey, M. J. and Douglas, K. M. (eds) *Feedback: The Communication of Praise, Criticism, and Advice* (pp. 265–278). New York: Peter Lang Publishing.

Hattie, J. and Timperley, H. (2007). The power of feedback. *Review of Educational Research*, 77(1), 81–112.

Katz, N. (2006). *Providing educational feedback*. The Association of Professors of Gynaecology and Obstetrics (APGO).

Keyton, J. (2005). *Communicating in Groups: Building Relationships for Effective Decision Making*, 3rd edn. New York: Oxford University Press.

Mory, E. H. (2004). Feedback research revisited. In: Jonassen, D. H. (ed) *Handbook of Research on Educational Communications and Technology*, 2nd edn (pp. 745–783). Mahwah, NJ: Lawrence Erlbaum Associates Publishers.

Price, M., Handley, K., Millar, J. and O'Donovan, B. (2010). Feedback: all that effort, but what is the effect? *Assessment & Evaluation in Higher Education*, 35(3), 277–289.

Race, P. (2001). *Using feedback to help students to learn*. The Higher Education Academy. Available at: https://phil-race.co.uk/wp-content/uploads/Using_feedback.pdf (accessed 21 April, 2017).

Sachdeva, A. K. (1996). Use of effective feedback to facilitate adult learning. *Journal of Cancer Education*, 11(2), 106–118.

Shrivastava, S. R., Shrivastava, P. S. and Ramasamy, J. (2014). Effective feedback: An indispensable tool for improvement in quality of medical education. *Journal of Pedagogical Development*, 4(1). Available at: www.beds.ac.uk/jpd/volume-4-issue-1/effective-feedback-an-indispensible-tool-for-improvement-in-quality-of-medical-education (accessed 29 August, 2016).

Sockalingam, N. (2012). Understanding adult learners' needs. *Faculty Focus*, 6 August. Available at: www.facultyfocus.com/articles/teaching-and-learning/understanding-adult-learners-needs/ (accessed 29 August, 2016).

University of Westminster (n.d.). *Learning from Feedback*. Available at: http://practiceexchange.westminster.ac.uk/Documents/LearningFromFeedback.pdf (accessed 29 June, 2017).

Vygotsky, L. S. (1978). *Mind in Society*. London: Harvard University Press.

Snapshot J: Demonstrating progress

Ask us to identify the training that we have either delivered or observed that might be considered 'outstanding' and you might be surprised by our response.

Yes, planning, pace and personality are very important!

Yes, creative teaching never fails to grab our attention (particularly Simon's)!

Yes, seeing participants being 'active' in training sessions is great.

But it is more about the *progress* that participants make in sessions that undoubtedly is at the heart of what we consider to be 'excellent training'. This is supported by Coe *et al.* who assert that 'progress is the yardstick by which [training] quality should be assessed' (2014: 2). In this Snapshot we respond to three key questions that others have asked us about this interesting focus:

1   'What does it mean when participants are "making progress" in one of our training sessions?' (Jackie)
2   'Why is it important that participants "make progress" in our training sessions?' (Hani)
3   'How can we quickly show the progress that participants are making during one of our training sessions?' (Gemma)

> **NOTE!**
> This Snapshot focusses on progress made during a training session and not over a period of time in which a 'unit of training' is delivered.

'What does it mean when participants are "making progress" in one of our training sessions?' (Jackie)

Ultimately, Jackie, it is about participants actually learning in your training session. This is very different to them simply attending your training ('being') or taking part in the activities you plan as part of the session ('doing') – just because they are there in body and are active does not necessarily mean they are learning anything! We understand participants to be making progress in training sessions when their knowledge base increases, their skills set improves, their understanding deepens, and/or their attitudes change. We believe that the best training facilitates development in most/all of these different aspects.

'Why is it important that participants "make progress" in our training sessions?' (Hani)

It's good practice, Hani! Your training should not simply give participants time off from their day job, nor should it be about having a nice lunch, or just enjoying listening to you speak. Instead, we strongly believe that the training you deliver should be driven by the notion of 'impact' – by this we mean positively influencing participants so that they can go back to their workplace and make valuable changes to both policy and practice for the benefit of those that they work with/support. This can be achieved by helping participants to see the progress they are making during your training so that they can 'clarify misconceptions and embed knowledge as understanding' (Bodmin College, n.d.: 2). You as the trainer can also benefit from this as it helps you 'to reshape and adapt learning activities to personalise [them] to suit individuals and groups more accurately, without capping the learning of others' (p. 2).

'How can we quickly show the progress that participants are making during one of our training sessions?' (Gemma)

Here are ten ideas, Gemma, that we particularly like using in our own training:

1   Invite participants to write a short 'Progress Slip' during the training session that clearly identifies something they have learned to date. Get them to review this at the end of the training – can they add anything else to the Slip?
2   Give participants a paper clock (circle) that is split into four quarters. Build in time for participants to record their 'learning journey' during different parts of the day (in different quarters) linked to shared success criteria that you display.
3   Pose questions to small groups throughout the training session that require participants to revisit your input and their own learning to successfully answer.
4   Offer opportunities for participants to peer-teach a skill/idea/strategy that has been introduced as part of your training input. Get peers to offer feedback on how well they understood what they have been taught.
5   Suggest that participants send a quick message (text, email, Facebook comment, Tweet) to one of their colleagues at their place of work that summarises the most important learning for them from the training to date.
6   Ask participants to write down a 'Killer Question' that they would not have been able to answer had they not engaged in different parts of your training session.
7   Give participants different grids, e.g. **QUADS** (**QU**estions, **A**nswers, **D**etails, **S**ource) to complete during your training session in an effort to record their 'learning in progress'.
8   Challenge participants to ask you questions based on the training content to monitor the progress that you (working-in-role) have made during the training so far.
9   Get participants to share extracts/photographs of work they have completed, reporting on the progress they have made in response to the success criteria and recommendations.
10   Let each participant record a verbal sentence or two onto their phone or your phone/tablet that summarises what they have learned so far in the session. Play the sentences back to see if there are similarities in different participants' learning.

There are, of course, many other ideas we could have included in the list above. We conclude this Snapshot with a small collection of our favourite activities to support participants in demonstrating progress in training sessions. Choose those you feel most comfortable using or adapt those you don't like to suit your training approach/style:

▪ Fill the brain – At the start of the training session get participants to draw the outline of a brain on a piece of paper. Every 20 minutes get them to record something inside the outline, 'filling the brain' with their learning.

- Reduction – Invite participants to demonstrate their learning part way through the session with just one word which they can verbally 'unpack' with a peer.
- Mind map – Suggest that participants mind map their prior knowledge of the training focus before the start of the session. With the support of your input, get participants to revisit this during the session, adding new knowledge and amending existing knowledge using a different coloured pen.
- Learning placemats – Visit http://tinyurl.com/zbqkopn, downloading and adapting the placemats that can be completed by participants during your training session.
- Answer me quick – Offer participants whiteboards and pens for them to record and show their answers to questions you ask them during the training to evaluate their progress, e.g. those that require an ABCD, T/F or Y/N response.

Table 10.4 Recommended readings and resources

Source	Title	Author/s	Year	Web link
Online PDF	Outstanding strategies for progress checking	Bodmin College	n.d.	http://tinyurl.com/hz6z2vn
Website	Ten easy ways to demonstrate progress in a lesson	Galloway	2014	http://tinyurl.com/jsdxba2

References

Bodmin College (n.d.). *Outstanding strategies for progress checking.* Available at: www.bodmincollege.co.uk/wp-content/uploads/2013/01/Progress-Check-Booklet-Single-Pages.pdf (accessed 1 July, 2016).

Coe, R., Aloisi, C., Higgins, S. and Major, L. E. (2014). *What makes great teaching? Review of the underpinning research.* London: Sutton Trust. Available at: www.suttontrust.com/wp-content/uploads/2014/10/What-makes-great-teaching-FINAL-4.11.14.pdf (accessed 1 July, 2016).

Chapter 11

Assessment

Alan says:

> The best thing about being a teacher (of adults or children) is the moment when a student says, 'Ah … I've never understood that before.' It's wonderful to witness in a child, and even more joyous in an adult, because they are often surprised that they can finally understand something that has eluded them in 45 years of life. This moment of clarity is far more likely to happen when there is some level of assessment involved.
>
> Last week I had a group of teachers doing some calculations involving standard form without calculators (for example, $10^8 \times 10^{-4}$). The simple assessment questions I used gave everyone involved validation that the process had worked: some teachers learned how to do it for the first time; those teachers that could already do these calculations had observed my way of explaining it. I then knew exactly when I could move on to the next topic. Both those teachers that had never understood how to do these calculations before, and those who had never understood the procedures they used, left buzzing with the excitement of understanding and increased confidence.

Imagine that you are a participant and the training you are attending has just started. The trainer who is delivering the session smiles, opens their mouth, and says:

'At the end of the training we are going to have a test to see how much you have learned!'

Question: How would you feel upon hearing this?

We suspect your response may be less than favourable!

We are mindful of the wealth of content that could be explored in this chapter introduction. To help focus our discussion, we have chosen to investigate four of the 'five [adapted] key principles of assessment derived from common premises of adult learning' (as identified by Kasworm and Marienau, 1997: 6) in an effort to highlight quality practices associated with the assessment **of** participants' learning ('at the end'). These are presented in Table 11.1.

> **NOTE!**
> This introduction touches slightly on assessment as learning (self/peer assessment) but does not focus on the assessment for participants' learning (formative). For clarification on these different types of assessment see http://tinyurl.com/zofda3o. If you seek guidance and advice on using the principles in Table 11.1 as part of your practice, then we recommend you invest in a copy of Vella *et al.*'s (1998) excellent book *How Do They Know They Know? Evaluating Adult Learning.*

Table 11.1 Principles of adult assessment

Key premises of adult learning		Key principles of adult-oriented assessment practice
Learning is derived from multiple sources.	1	Recognises multiple sources of knowing, that is, learning that occurs from interaction with a wide variety of informal and formal knowledge sources.
Learning engages the whole person and contributes to that person's development.	2	Recognises and reinforces the cognitive and affective domains of learning.
Learning and the capacity for self-direction are promoted by feedback.	3	Focusses on adults' active involvement in learning and assessment processes, including active engagement in self-assessment.
Learning occurs in context; its significance relates in part to its impact on those contexts.	4	Embraces adult learners' involvement in and impact on the broader world of work, family and community.

1. Recognises multiple sources of knowing, that is, learning that occurs from interaction with a wide variety of informal and formal knowledge sources

Good trainers appreciate that participants' learning cannot (and should not) just be assessed by a sit-down examination. We know from the likes of Lave and Wenger (1991) that effective learning can occur through the modelling of expert performance roles. What this means is that participants should be encouraged to show their competences through role play, demonstrations and performance opportunities. These can be simulated, i.e. take place in the training environment, or can take place in real-world contexts, e.g. the participants' working environment. These strategies allow participants to 'develop abilities that facilitate the "doing" of what they know through performance and action' (Kasworm and Marienau, 1997: 9). By practically applying what they have learned from their training, both trainer and participants should be able to ascertain strengths and weaknesses in their abilities from what is said and done; these can be established either through observations undertaken in the training environment or via oral presentations, videos or PowerPoint presentations that report on the outcomes of activity undertaken in the participants' working environment.

2. Recognises and reinforces the cognitive and affective domains of learning

When thinking about the assessment of participants' learning, an important consideration that you should be mindful of is what is actually being assessed, including:

▪ The **cognitive domain** (Bloom, 1956) – Learning related to knowledge
▪ The **affective domain** (Krathwohl *et al.*, 1964) – Learning related to attitudes, feelings and emotions.

Good trainers make effective use of the taxonomy of educational objectives for both domains (see Thomas, 2004) to help them (a) clarify the level they are assessing, and (b) use appropriate foundational verbs when formulating assessment tasks and associated success criteria. An example of this is offered in the following box:

> Broad learning aim – Thinking critically and making judgements (higher level).
>
> Assessment task – Produce a poster that compares and contrasts short-term strategies for managing the behaviour of learners with Attention Deficit Hyperactivity Disorder (ADHD).
>
> Success criteria (examples) – A balanced critique of each strategy is offered; discussion points are validated with reference to academic literature.

3. Focusses on adults' active involvement in learning and assessment processes, including active engagement in self-assessment

As opposed to assessment being done to participants, we believe that adult learners should be part of the process. A key way in which this can be achieved is through self-assessment that sees participants 'undertaking "objective" assessment of their own work' (Jones, 2005: 20) once completed. Good training involves participants being given opportunities to reflect critically on their work, identifying not only aspects of merit but also gaps in their own learning based on the criteria set for the assessment task. This reflection can be orally shared with trainers or peers, or can be added in written form to the end of their assessed work. Following this, you can then offer focussed feedback that helps to either validate or challenge participants' self-assessment in an effort to build their competences in self-review. A particularly effective strategy that we use in our own training is proposed by Jones (2005: 20):

> present [participants with] a series of anonymous learners' work, possibly from a previous cohort, so that they can review and evaluate work that does and does not meet the assessment criteria. This will clarify what has been required in a task/activity/assignment and lessons learnt can be applied to their own work.

4. Embraces adult learners' involvement in and impact on the broader world of work, family and community

Kasworm and Marienau assert that '[a]ssessment should help validate what adult learners apply in the various contexts of their lives' (1997: 12). When assessing participants, it is important for them to consider and report (where possible/appropriate) on the wide-ranging effects that the training has had as opposed to just limiting it to the participant and their immediate working environment. To help visualise this 'broader world of work, family, and community', we find the system levels proposed in Bronfenbrenner's (1995) Bioecological Systems Theory useful in helping participants to identify different 'entities' that could be influenced by their new knowledge/skills/understanding/attitudes. As a trainer, you should actively encourage participants to collect and report data using practical methods such as questionnaires, interviews, focus groups and observations in an effort to capture the impact noted at different levels. Good practice suggests that these findings should be presented in a variety of methods that help participants meet the objectives of the training, e.g. reports, portfolios, reflective papers, debates and journals. We particularly like allowing participants to decide on which assessment method they would like to use to demonstrate their learning. This helps them to feel that they have some control and ownership over their assessment; it can also promote a little creativity too!

In summary:

- Participants should be assessed through opportunities that allow them to 'put into practice' what they have learned. These can take place during the training or in their place of work.
- Trainers and participants need to be clear about what is actually being assessed, ensuring that this is explicitly linked to the success criteria set.
- Participants should be actively encouraged to self-assess their work as part of the assessment process.
- Assessment strategies offered to participants should allow them to consider the wide-ranging effect of changes they make to policy and practice and not solely focus on themselves and those they work directly with.
- Assessment sits alongside the activities you include in your training, and should be planned at the same time or before the activities are chosen. This can be seen in the *A-frame of training* (see Figure A, page 4).

Table 11.2 Recommended readings and resources

Source	Title	Author/s	Year	Web link
Paper	Course assessment practices and student learning strategies in online courses	Arend	2007	http://tinyurl.com/ycjnmh4u and click 'Download PDF'
Monograph	Evaluating professional development: A framework for adult education	Kutner *et al.*	1997	http://tinyurl.com/zmr2vy6
Pamphlet	The role of teachers in the assessment of learning	Assessment Reform Group	n.d.	http://tinyurl.com/yqfrsc

SOLO hexagons

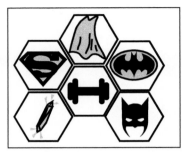

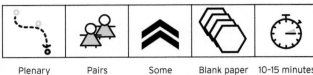

| Plenary | Pairs | Some preparation needed | Blank paper hexagons | 10-15 minutes |

Give each pair around 10-20 paper hexagons and ask participants to write down a key idea from your training on each hexagon. They have to then decide how the hexagons best link together, placing them next to other key ideas that are connected. **SOLO taxonomy** can be used to describe a participant's learning journey. They may start knowing almost nothing (pre-structural) but then they have an idea (uni-structural) or several ideas (multi-structural). Participants then begin to connect these ideas (relational). Once they are confident with some knowledge they can apply it to entirely new situations (extended abstract) (Biggs and Tang, 2007).

All of the ideas on this page and the next are based around promoting talk as a form of assessment.

Benefits
- This activity is designed to help participants spend time developing and discussing the connections between all of the ideas you have discussed to promote relational thinking, whilst you are able to assess and guide.

Considerations
- Participants must be able to justify any links they make and they are encouraged to make as many connections as possible.
- Try pairs that have not previously worked together throughout the rest of your training so that they are getting a fresh perspective on the activity.

Set-up tips
- Laminate the hexagons and use mini whiteboard pens so that you can reuse them afterwards.
- If you have got big enough tables, make the hexagons quite large (around 15cm across); this will enable you to read their work more easily.

After they have finished, go around and give participants more keywords to add to hexagons, e.g. words that relate to a future or a previous training session.

Ask participants to apply this knowledge to a completely new situation to promote **extended abstract** thinking.

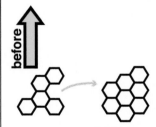

It can be a powerful activity to use both before and after your training to see the improvements in participants' confidence and their ability to make connections.

Newsroom interviews

Ask everybody to write three questions that link to the most important ideas from the day. Put the participants into two lines so that participants are facing one another. The participants on one side are the interviewers and on the other side they are the 'experts' being recorded for a news bulletin. It is then like a speed dating event with a pairing lasting for two minutes where the interviewers ask one, two or all three of their questions. The interviewers can push for more detail if they do not think the answers are good enough. After two minutes one of the lines moves one place to the left, and the other side ask their questions.

NEWS

Convincing cue cards

Prepare a range of keywords or key phrases on cue cards that are suitable for your training session; for example, subject knowledge, critical thinking, reflectiveness, understanding and compassion. Now pick an individual to talk to you for up to one minute about what they have achieved/demonstrated or improved compared to your chosen word/phrase. This is a good way of highlighting that training is not just about the subject knowledge, but often about developing the skills or judgement that participants have.

Alternative - If you have a large group you could split them up into groups of four or five and appoint one person to lead each smaller group.

Narrative

If the training involves an easily demonstrable skill, one nice way to embed the learning is to ask a pair of participants to work together as they perform the action. Whilst one person is 'doing it' the other narrates the process, explaining what is being done and why it is being done. It is therefore possible to assess both participants' understanding at the same time.

We begin compressions

Extension - Ask the group watching to feedback, first on the activity and then on whether any important points were missed out from the narration.

Questions using Socrative

| Plenary | Individuals | Some preparation needed | Good Wi-Fi connection, participant devices | 20 minutes |

Picture this scenario: You ask participants to log on to a web address you have given them using their smartphones, tablets or laptops. They select answers for a range of multiple-choice questions before going on to type in answers to written questions. Participants can then see everybody's answers and they can select the answer that is best. Socrative is an app/website (www.socrative.com) that can be used to create quizzes and manage all of the above. Whilst the most obvious usage may be to write simple multiple-choice questions, we believe the real power comes from asking open-ended questions that require written responses and giving participants time to discuss these before responding.

All of the ideas on this page and the next will be easier to understand if you log on to the websites.

Benefits
- For the uses described here, Socrative is free!
- It is easy for the trainer to see all of the answers by all of the participants. This enables you to assess if any individuals are struggling, but also to see if there are any topics you have covered that remain a weakness. You can also save the results of the quiz for later analysis.

Considerations
- You can choose to let participants go at the own rate (Student Paced), or you can choose when to move onto the next question (Teacher Paced).

Set-up tips
- You can change your electronic 'room name' – from something like 3303492934e to TrainingSusan, for example. To achieve this, click 'Menu' (this can be found at the top right of the dashboard).
- Responses can be anonymous or named.

You can write the quizzes (or the participants can) in Excel and then import them. This can save you quite a lot of time.

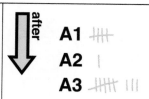

You can ask a 'Quick question' and get instant feedback. Participants can then vote on their favourite answer.

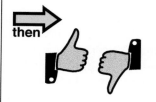

Why not use Socrative to ask questions about your training, e.g. did the training meet the learning objectives? How could the training be improved?

Presentations with questions – NearPod

NearPod is a presentation app/website (visit www.nearpod.com) that enables participants to follow the presentation on their own device. The real power comes from being able to embed questions into the presentation so that you can ensure that everyone has remained on task and understood what you have been saying. One innovative question type is a 'Drawing'. For the right question, a drawing answer can be a very powerful assessment tool (for example, 'Draw butane' or 'Label the sections of the skull'), and you as the presenter can see everybody's drawings at the same time, and then send the best (or worst) of these out to all of the participants.

Participant videos with Educreations

Educreations is an app/website (visit www.educreations.com) that enables you to create and then share videos with drawings, text and pictures alongside a recorded commentary. However, you can also use it to give participants a way of creating a brief synopsis of the training, which you can then use to assess if they have met the learning aims. It is fairly intuitive to use but it will take participants a while to create a video. Their video will be better if you can ask them to answer specific questions.

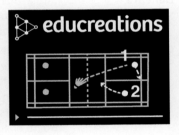

Note - In its simplest format Educreations is free to use; if you want to save all of the participants' videos then there is a fee.

Plickers feedback

A strategy we frequently use in our training is to ask a question and all the participants hold up a mini-whiteboard with their answer on it. However, you can use the Plickers app (visit www.plickers.com) to achieve the same thing and more, e.g. participants hold up a special piece of paper (that you have printed in advance) with black squares on it and the direction they hold it up dictates whether they have selected A, B, C or D. Take a photo of the whole group using the Plickers app and it will tell you who got each question right and wrong; you can also save the results. Plickers restricts you to multiple-choice questions but it only needs one smartphone for a whole class assessment. Because the squares appear random, participants cannot copy one another.

Summary spirals

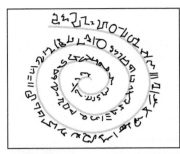

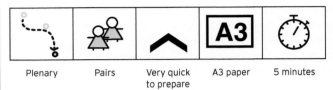

| Plenary | Pairs | Very quick to prepare | A3 paper | 5 minutes |

The summary spiral is a quick method for participants to work out what the key learning ideas have been for them. They draw a spiral on a piece of large paper and then write/ draw what the key messages have been for them from your session. The most important idea goes in the very centre of the spiral. Other shapes are available and may be more applicable to your training; these include pyramids, chains, pie charts, stepping stones and jigsaws.

All of the ideas on these pages (172–173) encourage participants to summarise their learning in a way that can be easily self-, peer- or trainer-assessed.

Benefits ▪ Rather than just asking participants to summarise your training, you are ensuring that the participants are thinking more deeply because they are forced to rate the importance of the ideas.

Considerations ▪ Although it can work well as an individual task, having another person to 'bounce ideas off' is usually more engaging and the discussion may help participants recall more of the course content.
▪ If the main reason for doing this activity is so that you can assess the participants' understanding, you may not want them in groups larger than two, to ensure everyone contributes.

Set-up tips ▪ A4 sized paper is big enough for individual work; A3 works well for pairs.

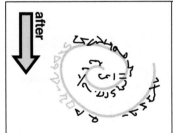

Ask participants to highlight their most challenging aspect of the learning – it may well not be the same as the key message in the centre of the spiral.

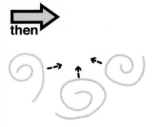

You (and others) can walk around the training room and compare what the key ideas are; these can be fed into a group summary. If everyone agrees, this should be quite quick!

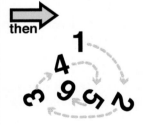

Once you have a summary spiral, you can create a *next-steps* spiral, where participants have to identify what their key actions are going to be after the training.

Sandwich-board summary

Get some large card and thread some string around the top to create a sandwich board. Each participant has to write on their board between one and three main learning points from the day (possibly with illustrations). Once they have finished, they put the sandwich board over their head and walk around the room, preaching their message as the truth in an attempt to try to convert others to agree with them!

Just a minute

Based on the popular BBC Radio 4 series, the idea is simple. Participants must talk for 60 seconds without deviation, hesitation or repetition on a topic of your choosing. They are allowed to repeat the words from the topic card but may not use other words more than once. The other participants must listen carefully and can 'buzz in' if the person speaking makes a mistake. If a participant makes a correct challenge, then they take over the topic and try to speak for the remaining time. This is a fun but challenging game; participants may not communicate all their ideas in a minute. You may wish to relax the rules at the end of 60 seconds and give participants an opportunity to add anything that was missed.

Video news-bite

We can take advantage of the fact that most participants will have cameras on their phones by asking small groups to create a news-style video clip at the end of the session that summarises what they have learned. Usually this should be a maximum of 60 seconds. You should be quite specific about what you want each group to focus on and you may also want to give each of the groups a slightly different topic. It is nice to share the clips with the whole group; if you have access to fast Wi-Fi the easiest way may be to ask participants to email them to you.

Alternative – You could ask individual participants to create these video clips at home which will encourage continuity in their learning.

Word splat

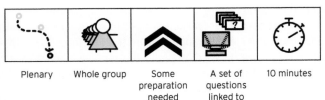

Plenary   Whole group   Some preparation needed   A set of questions linked to words, a projector   10 minutes

Many teachers will be familiar with the idea of word splat, but adult learners enjoy it too. Divide everybody into two teams which stand in two lines with one representative next to the projector from each side. A series of words are projected onto the board and you ask a series of questions which you (or they) have prepared in advance. The active player has to splat (hit) the board when they know the answer. You need to judge whose hand hits the board first and award a point. The players then swap for the next question and the team with the most points wins.

All of the ideas on this page and the next are based around questioning participants.

Benefits	▪ It is quick to organise and run, and is usually very engaging.
Considerations	▪ It is easy to write questions that only require a fairly superficial recall to answer; constructing questions which require deeper thought is more time-consuming.
	▪ Each question only tests two people at once so it is fairly limited in terms of assessing all participants.
Set-up tips	▪ If you have a 'know-it-all' in your group, why not appoint them as the quiz master?!
	▪ If you are skilled at using PowerPoint you can give your words custom animations to make them move around, which adds an extra element of tension to the proceedings.

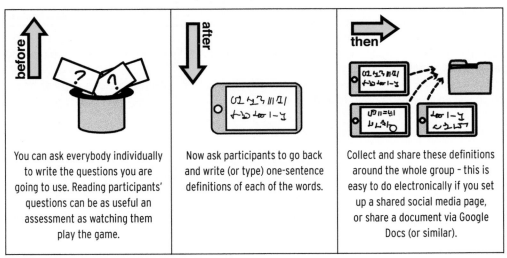

before You can ask everybody individually to write the questions you are going to use. Reading participants' questions can be as useful an assessment as watching them play the game.

after Now ask participants to go back and write (or type) one-sentence definitions of each of the words.

then Collect and share these definitions around the whole group – this is easy to do electronically if you set up a shared social media page, or share a document via Google Docs (or similar).

Loop dominoes

A simple way to check that participants can remember definitions (or can answer simple questions) is to create a series of loop dominoes where each domino card has a definition (or question) on the right and an answer to a different definition on the left. When participants are given the full set of dominoes they should be able to create a complete loop that correctly matches all of the definitions to their answers.

Alternative – If you have a similar number of people to domino pieces, you can deal them out amongst the whole group and participants will have to move themselves to form a loop.

Sewing cards

Get participants to work in small groups. Each group is given a piece of card you have prepared in advance that has two columns of holes down the middle (around 5–15). Down the left-hand side, next to every hole, participants have to write a question; on the right-hand side they write the answers that are jumbled up in order. Once they have written all the questions/answers they swap their card with another group. Give each team a long piece of wool that they have to use to 'sew' the questions to the answers.

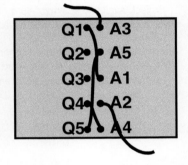

Pub quiz

There are clearly many ways to run a quiz as part of an assessment. If, however, you do not have a requirement to assess every individual then we can learn a lot by looking at the most successful pub quizzes. Include around 20 per cent easy questions and 20 per cent difficult ones with the remainder somewhere in the middle. Give teams duplicate answer sheets so that they can keep a copy of their answers, giving the other copy to another team to mark. If you can do a picture round or a 'labelling a diagram' round, then that will add to the variety. Alcohol is optional!

Remember – To avoid disputes your answer is always right, even when it's wrong.

References

Assessment Reform Group (n.d.). *The role of teachers in the assessment of learning*. London: Institute of Education. Available at: http://tinyurl.com/yqfrsc (accessed 23 May, 2017).

Biggs, J. and Tang, C. (2007). *Teaching for Quality Learning at University*, 3rd edn. Buckingham: SRHE and Open University Press.

Bloom, B. S. (1956). *Taxonomy of Educational Objectives. Handbook I: The Cognitive Domain*. New York: David McKay Co.

Bronfenbrenner, U. (1995). The bioecological model from a life course perspective: reflections of a participant observer. In: Moen, P., Elder, G. H. Jr. and Luscher, K. (eds) *Examining Lives in Context* (pp. 599–618). Washington, DC: American Psychological Association.

Jones, C. A. (2005). *Assessment for learning*. London: Learning and Skills Development Agency.

Kasworm, C. and Marienau, C. (1997). Principles for assessment of adult learning. *New Directions for Adult and Continuing Education*, 75, 5-16.

Krathwohl, D. R., Bloom, B. S. and Masia, B. B. (1964). *Taxonomy of Educational Objectives: Handbook II: Affective Domain*. New York: David McKay Co.

Kutner, M., Sherman, R., Tibbetts, J. and Condelli, L. (1997). *Evaluating professional development: A framework for adult education*. Building Professional Development Partnerships for Adult Educators Project. Available at: www.calpro-online.org/pubs/evalmon.pdf (accessed 23 May, 2017).

Lave, J. and Wenger, E. (1991). *Situated Learning: Legitimate Peripheral Participation*. Cambridge: Cambridge University Press.

Thomas, K. (2004). Learning Taxonomies in the Cognitive, Affective and Psychomotor Domains. *Rocky Mountain Alchemy*. Available at: www.rockymountainalchemy.com/whitePapers/rma-wp-learning-taxonomies.pdf (accessed 2 September, 2016).

Vella, J., Berardinelli, P. and Burrow, J. (1998). *How Do They Know They Know? Evaluating Adult Learning*. San Francisco: Jossey-Bass.

Snapshot K: Revision

One of the first questions you will probably ask yourself about revision is: 'Should I even allow any time for revision during my training sessions?' This is a great question and one that we will not answer! We believe that you will make that judgement by knowing the group you have in front of you, how much content you have to cover, how much time you have, and how essential it is that your participants can recall everything you have discussed during your training. However, even if you conclude that you will not put an 'explicit chunk of time' aside for revision, it may well be that you can squeeze in small activities that help to recap previous topics. This can make the training sessions feel more connected, as well as ensuring that participants are definitely remembering your key messages.

The brain

Before we talk about which pedagogical strategies seem to be most effective as revision techniques, let us first ask ourselves a few questions about how the brain works.

> WARNING! The next few paragraphs are not written by psychologists, nor are they written for neuroscientists: it is a high-level overview that provides us with a context for the revision techniques ... please stick with it!

Our brain is made up of 100 billion neurons and these are interconnected to many other neurons. The complexity of our brain is caused by the 100 trillion connections shared between our neurons and it is this tangled web that combines to form the unique structure of our brain. The neurons share an important trait with muscles: if we use them more they can become stronger and faster. At a biological level, frequently used pathways between neurons become reinforced by a myelin sheath; this speeds up the rate of transmission. The more times we access an idea, the easier we will find it to access that idea in the future.

However, it is a little bit more subtle than that. There are differences between activities that put ideas into our brain's long-term storage systems (reading an interesting article, for example) and activities that take ideas out of the brain's long-term storage (talking about it in depth, for example). When you need knowledge, whether it is to answer a question in an exam or a situation that you have to deal with, the neurological pathway that is important is our ability to recall the idea. So, when it comes to revision, we need to be practising pathways involved in recalling ideas rather than just trying to memorise them.

This can be seen in our layman's diagram of how the brain works (see Figure 11.1, inspired by Jones, 2014): the recall pathway (coloured) going back from long-term to working memory is what we need to be exercising most when it comes to revision.

> Don't believe us? We bet that you will recall more of this Snapshot if you go and discuss it with someone straight after reading it as opposed to you just reading it and not thinking about it again for a couple of days.

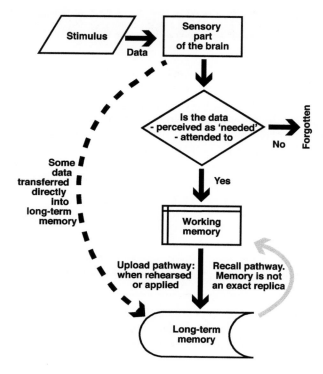

FIGURE 11.1 The pathways of data in the brain

How do adults learn differently to children?

During childhood, there are several key biological ideas that transform how the brain develops: there is significant myelination where grey cells are converted to white cells as the important pathways become reinforced. There is also significant synaptic pruning during early childhood and adolescence where unused connections between parts of the brain are reduced. Both of these events help a child's brain to develop and be efficient, enabling the child to fit into its environment.

Neither myelination nor synaptic pruning occurs at the same rate in an adult's brain. Therefore, whilst children learn all the time and pick up ideas relatively easily, for adults to learn something new they first need to perceive the ideas as being relevant or of interest to them.

So, how will this affect your revision strategies?

One recent piece of research brilliantly collates and summarises a list of strategies that are most successful as revision techniques. Dunlosky *et al.* (2013) undertook a meta-analysis where the results from over 300 other pieces of research were combined to reach an overall conclusion about what represents the most successful revision strategies that students can undertake by themselves.

The strategies that are likely to have a **high** level of impact are:

◾ Distributed practice – At a fundamental level we believe this is the most obvious but the most important: the more we revisit ideas the more likely we are to recall it at a later date. You may well have seen Figure 11.2 before: it shows how by revisiting a topic at A and B someone will have better recall of that topic in the future. Also, by revisiting an idea, not only do we 'top-up' the learning but after several 'top-ups' we see the rate at which we forget decrease. At its most basic, this is why a single training session is likely to be less effective than a series of inter-linked sessions or a single session which has quality pre-course engagement and post-course follow-up.

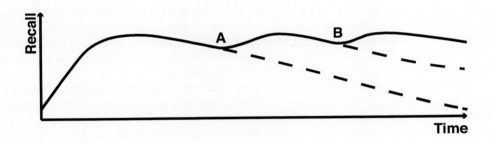

FIGURE 11.2 Distributed practice improving recall

◾ Practice testing – This is the process of frequently checking that you can recall all of the facts about a certain topic. This can take many forms, such as having a set of question and answer index cards or by covering up parts of a book and frequently trying to recall the facts.

These strategies have a **medium** impact:

◾ Self-explanation – When trying to learn something, think out loud about why it works, if there are any mistakes/problems you can identify or if specific solutions to a problem may work.
◾ Interleaved practice – This works just as well for physical activities as it does for answering questions. If you are practising something, rather than keep doing the same type of question (or activity) again and again before changing to the next type, it is better to mix them up. So, rather than doing AAA, BBB, CCC it is preferable to 'interleave' the questions: ABCBACCBA. For example, if you were doing some training on grammar, do not ask five questions about apostrophes, five questions on the use of colons and then five questions about full stops; do the questions in a random order.
◾ Elaborative interrogation – By understanding how something works, we are more likely to be able to recall it later.

But as well as seeing what works well, we should be aware of which strategies are likely to have a **low** impact; these include:

- Highlighting text
- Rereading
- Summarisation
- Keyword mnemonics
- Imagery.

This is not to say that there is not a place for the low-impact techniques: they often form a great starting point for learning and will have some impact, but they should not be used in isolation.

We can attempt to make links between these pedagogical conclusions and the ideas about how the brain works, and we can see that higher-impact techniques such as distributed practice, practice testing and interleaved practice all involve recalling ideas from the brain, but the low-impact techniques just upload them. Self-explanation and elaborative interrogation may be successful because they are using links to existing ideas and connections that already exist within our brains. The more effective revision strategies can be harder to plan for and support than the less effective ones (for example, it is harder to support a group of participants that are each doing different interleaved questions than participants that are all trying to answer the same questions), but the payoff is likely to be larger.

If you have time in your training, and it is appropriate for your audience, one of the most helpful things we can do as trainers is to help participants to understand which revision strategies are likely to be most effective and why.

In conclusion, there are several ways that we can encourage our participants to engage in more effective revision techniques:

- You can 'teach an old dog new tricks' but participants have to perceive those tricks as being relevant or of interest to them, and they should be supported through a series of effective recall-based learning strategies.
- Giving time over a series of sessions to revisit the key ideas is the best way to embed those ideas. This is an idea built around distributed practice.
- Do not assume that all participants are equally well-versed in effective revision techniques – share the understanding of what works well, and what does not.

Table 11.3 Recommended readings and resources

Source	Title	Author/s	Year	Web link
Article	Strengthening the student toolbox: Study strategies to boost learning	Dunlosky	2013	http://tinyurl.com/hykwh22

References

Dunlosky, J. (2013). Strengthening the student toolbox. *American Educator*, Fall, 12–21.

Dunlosky, J., Rawson, K., Marsh, E., Nathan, M. and Willingham, D. (2013). Improving students' learning with effective learning techniques: Promising directions from cognitive and educational psychology. *Psychological Science in the Public Interest*, 134(1), 4–58.

Jones, S. (2014). *Effective Revision Skills*. Presentation given at Cambourne Village College, Cambourne, Cambridge, February.

Chapter 12

Making an impact

> Alan says:
>
> **"** Many teachers like me will just fall into teacher training. It will not necessarily be something that you always wanted to do, but is something that you were asked to do one day, and then years later you are still doing it and loving it. I often get asked if I miss teaching children, and other teachers often seem surprised/disappointed when I answer 'No'. I love my job now, but the teachers I meet on a daily basis are likely to make all the same mistakes as my pupils; they have the same sense of fun and silliness, and the same sense of wonder as they learn something that they have not understood or been able to do before. Teachers can also be just as easily distracted as children, and I need to employ many similar behaviour management strategies (see Snapshot F).
>
> The only thing I miss is the ability to build up meaningful relationships with pupils, and to form a pastoral bond with them – my work with teachers is rarely over a long a period of time, so those relationships do not develop to the same extent. Therefore, where possible, I like to be involved in programmes that involve some sustained engagement: it is much more satisfying as a trainer to see genuine progress being made by teachers than to just witness short-term gains and to be left to imagine the impact it will have on students. **"**

We're going to let you in on a little secret. Do you want to hear what it is? If so, come a bit closer to your page or screen. If you are lucky enough to be listening to us on audio book, then move your ear closer to the speaker and turn us up.

Bit closer.

Just a bit more.

There – that's enough.

Okay … here's the secret …

> No matter how much preparation you put into your training, no matter how brilliant your delivery, no matter how engaged your participants are, your training is likely to only have a small impact on their practice.

Bet you wish we had not told you that now, eh?

If the above is indeed true, knowing this is likely to get you questioning why this professional book has been written; after all, there does not seem to be any point in running quality training if it is not going to have much impact. Unfortunately we have seen it all too often: participants leave training sessions empowered and promise they are going to make changes to their practice based on their learning from the training. But once they return to their workplace their enthusiasm begins to wane and other work pressures remain in place. All too quickly they go back to the ways they have always done things. Indeed, Yasin *et al.* suggest that 'less than 15 to 20 per cent of the knowledge and skills acquired in trainings [is] actually applied in the workplace' (2014: 179). This chapter introduction is written to counter the above, specifically exploring how it is possible to ensure that the training you deliver does have an impact and that participants do deliver on their promises. In the *A-frame of training* (see Figure A, page 4) we see there are two strands that we need to consider to get the maximum impact from the session: for participants to engage in a meaningful action plan, and for the participants to be given high-quality after-care. We begin by considering what we mean by 'impact'.

Nashashibi (2004: 3) offers a definition which we particularly like:

> Impact is an inclusive term covering the overall effect of learning provision on those it is designed to benefit – the [participants] and potential learners and the communities in which they live or work. It therefore includes the effect that the learning process has had on the [participants] and, through their progress or endeavours, on other people.

When thinking about the nature of this 'effect', you should be mindful that this could be negative (resulting in poorer job performance) or zero (no effect on job performance). However, the training we know that you will deliver as a result of engaging with this book is likely to result in a positive effect, e.g. a wider knowledge base, an improved skills-set, a deeper understanding and constructive attitudes (KSUA). Despite this, none of these changes will have any impact on policy or practice if they are not utilised by participants. This mirrors the third level of Kirkpatrick's (1959) Four-Level Model of Training Evaluation, which focusses on the transfer of KSUA from the training context to the workplace. Yes, it is important to know how participants have reacted to your training (Level 1 of Kirkpatrick's model); yes, it is crucial to know that some kind of learning has taken place (Level 2), but we are more interested (for the purposes of this chapter introduction) in how participants have applied their new KSUA. This application can be achieved in a variety of ways, examples of which include:

- Direct use of new skills in one's daily practice.
- Informal discussions with co-workers during breaks and lunchtime periods.
- Modelling strategies for peers to observe in situ through coaching and mentoring opportunities.
- Sharing new knowledge with colleagues through team meetings, training sessions or paper-based summary reports.
- Creating a small display of learning in the staff area for co-workers to read and reflect on.

Interestingly, the issue is not necessarily how participants have applied their KSUA but whether they have actually been encouraged to do so in the first place. Grossman and Salas (2011) claim that participants are unlikely to transfer new knowledge and skills to their job unless their work environment encourages them to do so. This encouragement is seemingly facilitated by four specific factors, as identified in Figure 12.1 by Cromwell and Kolb (2004).

It will probably come as no surprise to you that those participants 'who ... receiv[ed] high levels of organisation, supervisor and peer support, and who also participated in a peer support network, reported higher levels of transfer of knowledge and skills' (Krishnamani and Haider, 2012: 81). The support of the workplace is thus essential if participants are going to make any impact with the KSUA they have learned from your training. Whilst this is largely 'out of your hands', there are several ways that you can actively 'trigger' this support:

- Send a letter to the participant's 'boss', reminding them of the training the participant has attended and thanking them in advance for their support in encouraging the participant to utilise their new KSUA.

- Make a call (telephone, Skype, in person) to members of the senior management team, asking them about the impact the participant's training has had on the department.
- Email or meet with participants to ascertain what opportunities they have had or are planning to capitalise on to transfer their learning for the benefit of the workplace.

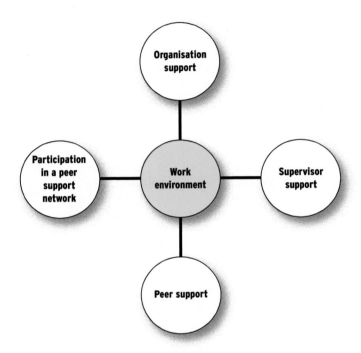

FIGURE 12.1 Factors that may help encourage participants to use their new skills and knowledge in the work environment

Clearly, timing is an important consideration when utilising the above: deploy them too early and responses are likely to be minimal; too late and the impact will have been long forgotten. A useful idea is to encourage participants near the end of your training to formulate a plan (ideally written but also can be verbal) that details the proposed actions of participants on their return to their workplace with a timeframe as to when these actions will be notionally completed. You can then use this as a way of helping you to plan the best time to make contact with individuals at the participants' workplace.

Ultimately, through this contact you will want to know how the training has had an impact on the participants and others with whom they work. The examples below have been adapted from the University of South Alabama (n.d.: 14-15) for relevance to education contexts:

- improved quality of work in terms of learning and teaching
- higher productivity (both learners and teachers)
- reduction in staff turnover
- improved quality of work/life balance
- improved human relations between different stakeholders in the education setting

- fewer parent/carer grievances
- lower absenteeism
- higher learner/teacher morale
- greater job satisfaction
- increased pupil/student attainment.

But how can we know that this impact has actually occurred? Nashashibi suggests that 'impact is essentially about "before" and "after"' (2004: 34). Participants should therefore be encouraged to gather both quantitative (numbers) and qualitative (narrative) information to help them ascertain the difference (the impact) between these two points. This evidence can be amassed in a variety of ways, as highlighted by Burton *et al.* (2014) (see Table 12.1):

Table 12.1 Techniques that may help provide evidence for impact

Test results	Document analysis	Observations	Interview transcripts
Questionnaire findings	Diary/journal extracts	Focus group discussions	

Many educators are likely to be familiar with these methods of data collection due to the surge of practitioner research and enquiry taking place in educational settings to help 'inform professional practice and organisational decision-making' (Scott and McNeish, 2013: 5). The effects of participants' applied KSUA, be it positive, negative or zero, should be evident when comparing the 'starting point' and 'end point' data they have collected. You may wish to signpost participants to the comprehensive works of Taylor-Powell (1996) and Taylor-Powell and Renner (2003) in helping them to effectively analyse their data.

In summary:

- Your training can have a positive, negative or zero effect on participants' performance.
- Impact relates not only to the participants who attend your training but those individuals that participants work with (directly or indirectly).
- Participants need the support of their workplace in order to transfer their learning. This needs to be encouraged in time-appropriate ways.
- Impact can be measured through the analysis of words and numbers. This data can be gathered through a range of data collection methods.

Table 12.2 Recommended readings and resources

Source	Title	Author/s	Year	Web link
White Paper	Beyond smiley sheets: Measuring the ROI of learning and development	Bennington and Laffoley	2012	http://tinyurl.com/zlhauor
Literature review	The evaluation of learning and development in the workplace: A review of the literature	Mavin, Lee and Robson	2010	http://tinyurl.com/h3g3weu
Report	Kirkpatrick and Beyond: A Review of Models of Training Evaluation	Tamkin, Yarnall and Kerrin	2002	http://tinyurl.com/j6b8jjy

Synopticator

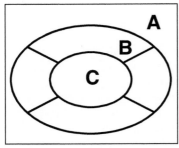

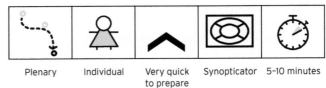

Plenary   Individual   Very quick to prepare   Synopticator   5–10 minutes

One of the simplest ways to improve the impact of your training is ensure that all participants create an action plan about what will change for them as a result of your course. A nice way to lay this out is on a single A4 page template for their synopsis and action plan, something that we call the 'Synopticator'. Encourage participants to write or doodle anything related to the day around the outside of the paper (A). The new ideas, or most important considerations from the course for each participant go in the outer part of the ellipse (B). Finally, in the middle, participants write an action plan (C). This idea is based upon the course 'nutshell', as used by the Science Learning Network (see Bevins *et al.*, 2011: 9).

Benefits	Although participants may well have a range of other printed materials to take back with them, this is a single sheet that can either go in their diary or on their wall by their desk as a frequently seen reminder of the training.
Considerations	The actions do not have to apply directly to the participant: it is quite possible that the actions are for the participant's manager or people that work for/with them.
	Many training courses we have delivered lend themselves really clearly to a single-page synopsis and action plan. Some courses, however, especially those that last more than one day, do not fit well on a single piece of paper; for these you may wish instead to just focus on the action plan.
Set-up tips	Participants really should complete the Synopticator individually as the main point is that it should be personal to them. Everyone should have got something out of your training, but there is likely to be a different emphasis for each person.

Do not leave it until the end of the day to begin the Synopticator for whole-day training courses. Give participants time before break-times and lunch to begin working on it.

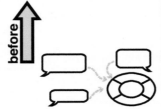

Before participants write their Synopticator, ask the participants to verbally summarise your course to remind everyone what has been covered.

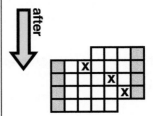

Ask participants to commit to dates for each of the actions they have given themselves and to write these in their diaries.

Follow-up interview

Around six weeks after the training, ask participants to reflect how the training and their action plan has had an impact on them and any other people that are affected by it. This is often easiest to collate through a paper or electronic form, but it is even better if you can talk to the participants directly. Ask participants to prepare for the chat by telling them that it will be short (around five minutes) but that you want to hear about any successes that they have had as a result of your course or plans they have for the future. This will actively encourage participants to take responsibility for implementing changes as a result of the training.

Horoscope

A fun alternative to writing an action plan is to ask participants to write a horoscope about what the future holds for them in their work. This ensures participants are positive about the future but you may need to remind them that any improvements for the future will not just happen; they will have to be active to implement changes in their own practice.

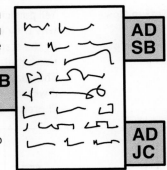

Single-page summary

If you are working with a team that normally work together you may wish to create a single poster that summarises the training that you have delivered that day. Once they have completed the poster, participants then need to write on large sticky notes the actions that apply to them. This poster can then be hung up in a shared area as a constant reminder of the actions that everyone has to undertake for the whole team to succeed. Try to use paper that is A2 or larger for the summary to give participants enough space to add sticky notes later.

Segueing from training to doing

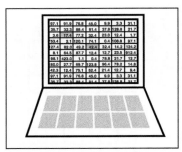

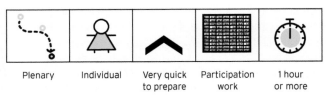

| Plenary | Individual | Very quick to prepare | Participation work | 1 hour or more |

For many training courses it may be appropriate for participants to bring along a piece of work that is linked to the course aims that they can complete, or at least begin, on the day of the training. Examples we have used for educators in the past include data analysis, creating action plans and timelines, writing replies to challenging parents/carers and reviewing existing or planning new schemes of work. However, anything that can be easily brought to the training room and can be efficiently worked upon should be considered. As a part of two-week or four-week training courses, we have spent whole mornings or afternoons with participants, helping to support them as they analyse data and write development plans.

Benefits	■ We can encourage all participants to be reflective on the training if participants do a productive part of their jobs within the training room, using what they have just learned.
	■ This can work really well at the end of a day's training.
Considerations	■ All the resources required by participants need to be high quality if this is going to feel like an effective use of your training time. Participants will feel very frustrated if they could have performed the same tasks more quickly where they normally work.
Set-up tips	■ Tell participants in advance what they need to bring along on the day and why they will need it.
	■ At the start of your training check that participants have brought everything that they will need: do not wait until the point when they need it! This may give them (or you) time to fetch what they have forgotten but it will also enable you to plan an alternative if someone arrives completely ill-prepared.

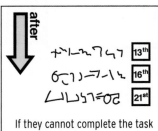

If they cannot complete the task on the day, ask participants to break down their next steps alongside dates and relevant ideas from your training.

If they manage to complete the task on the day, ask participants to state how the task outcome has been influenced by their participation in the training.

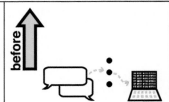

Before they start their individual tasks, ask participants to spend five minutes looking at their tasks together and coming up with a three bullet point mini-plan.

Colleagues with benefits!

Participants write down a short list of the groups of people that benefit from them doing their job well (for educators this may be pupils/students, colleagues and parents/carers). Participants then write down the name of an individual from each of these groups; they can make up this name or use a real person as an example. For each of these identified individuals, participants need to write how they will benefit from the training they have attended and what participants need to do to make this happen.

	Kenny (Student)	Dr G (Parent)	Mrs Cooper (Colleague)
Benefits			
Actions			

Timeline

Each participant prepares a timeline, identifying points when they will be able to complete a task that has been a focus of your training and a point at which they should be able to assess if their work has been successful. This will encourage participants not only to take responsibility for their successes but also to think about how they may be able to measure impact.

Alternative – If you are training a group that works together it may make sense to have a common timeline and ask individuals to sign up to different parts.

Shout it out

Encourage participants to share what they have learned on your training and what they will be doing next as a result. This could be through a Facebook/Instagram/Snapchat posting, an internal web page, or even just as a small A5 poster that they pin up on their work noticeboard. If they share what they have learned as a result of the training, participants are more likely to commit to a change, and they are more likely to engage in an informal conversation with their colleagues for the benefit of everyone.

References

Bennington, K. and Laffoley, T. (2012). *Beyond smiley sheets: Measuring the ROI of learning and development. Report.* Chapel Hill, NC: UNC Kenan-Flagler Business School. Available at: http://tinyurl.com/zlhauor (accessed 1 June, 2017).

Bevins, S. C., Jordan, J. and Perry, E. (2011). Reflecting on professional development. *Educational Action Research*, 19(3), 399–411.

Burton, N., Brundrett, M. and Jones, M. (2014). *Doing Your Education Research Project*, 2nd edn. London: Sage.

Cromwell, S. E. and Kolb, J. K. (2004). An examination of work-environment support factors affecting transfer of supervisory skill training in the workplace. *Human Resource Development Quarterly*, 15(4), 449–471.

Grossman, R. and Salas, E. (2011). The transfer of training: what really matters. *International Journal of Training and Development*, 15(2), 103–120.

Kirkpatrick, D. L. (1959). Techniques for evaluating training programs. *Journal of American Society for Training and Development*, 11, 1–13.

Krishnamani, S. and Haider, Y. (2012). Transfer of learning. *International Journal of Human Resource Management and Research*, 2(3), 73–94.

Mavin, S., Lee, L. and Robson, F. (2010). *The evaluation of learning and development in the workplace: A review of the literature.* London: Higher Education Funding Council for England. Available at: www.northumbria.ac.uk/static/5007/hrpdf/hefce/hefce_litreview.pdf (accessed 1 June, 2017).

Nashashibi, P. (2004). *The alchemy of learning: impact and progression in adult learning.* London: Learning and Skills Development Agency.

Scott, S. and McNeish, D. (2013). *School leadership evidence review: Using research evidence to support school improvement.* London: DfE.

Tamkin, P., Yarnall, J. and Kerrin, M. (2002). *Kirkpatrick and Beyond: A Review of Models of Training Evaluation.* Brighton: The Institute for Employment Studies.

Taylor-Powell, E. (1996). *Analyzing Quantitative Data.* Lancaster, WI: University of Wisconsin-Extension.

Taylor-Powell, E. and Renner, M. (2003). *Analyzing Quantitative Data.* Lancaster, WI: University of Wisconsin-Extension.

University of South Alabama (n.d.). *The Kirkpatrick Model of Training Evaluation.* Available at: www.southalabama.edu/coe/bset/johnson/660lectures/Kirk1.doc (accessed 8 August, 2016 though no longer available on 21 April, 2017).

Yasin, R. M., Faizal Amin Nur, Y., Ridzwan, C. R., Mohd Bekri, R., Azwin Arif, A. R., Irwan Mahazir, I. and Tajul Ashikin, H. (2014). Learning transfer at skill institutions' and workplace environment: A conceptual framework. *Asian Social Science*, 10(1), 179–188. Available at: www.ccsenet.org/journal/index.php/ass/article/view/33131 (accessed 12 August, 2016).

Snapshot L: Moving from teaching children to teaching adults

For a minute, pretend that you are Nathan ...

You have been teaching geography at secondary school for seven years and you love your job. You find it a tiring role but the rewards outweigh the demands. You feel that you are doing a good job and, because you are a reflective practitioner, you are always looking for ways to improve your lessons. There is nothing that fazes you at school – not the Year 11 bottom set on a Friday afternoon, nor asking the reprographics guy to print a class-set of maps with only five minutes' notice. You have been a subject leader for a few years, which was intimidating at first but now this does not provide you with too much of a problem, even when you have to cover for two teachers on a Monday morning during the staff briefing. Your head teacher has now asked you to run a series of six twilight sessions for a group of geography teachers within your Multi Academy Trust.

What do you do next?

First, we hope you say 'Yes!' Second, we hope you pick up a copy of this book. And most important, we hope you do not panic!

Nathan's situation is very similar to that of many teachers around the country as schools are increasingly being expected to run and deliver school-based training, whether this is Initial Teacher Training, or continuing professional support for teachers who are already in post. Our colleagues who have been in the same situation as Nathan (as we were at one point) are often nervous at first, and will re-plan their first sessions time and time again. But in our experience, all teachers have found the opportunity to be less intimidating and more rewarding than initially feared. Indeed, with a little support and guidance, teachers nearly always want to do more adult training once they have started!

There is an academic debate that has been running for over 40 years about the differences in teaching adults (referred to as andragogy) and children/young people (referred to as pedagogy). The difference between these terms is a topic of discussion we have avoided in this book, partly as we see this falling out of the remit of the book, partly because the word pedagogy is often used to refer to the teaching of anyone, but mainly because we think to rigidly separate the two ideas will obscure the similarities they share. A concise summary of much of the academic literature exploring both the differences and similarities between andragogy and pedagogy has been compiled by Holmes and Abington-Cooper (2000). Our overall position on the debate between andragogy and pedagogy can be summarised by the following statements:

1   Lessons learned in the school classroom will help improve adult training.
2   Lessons learned from adult training will help improve the school classroom.

Many of the activities contained in this book validate the first statement as these are activities that we initially used with children and young people but that we now successfully use to engage, motivate and assess adult learners. To defend the second statement, we look at the work of Knowles (1973) who wrote the seminal work *The Adult Learner: A Neglected Species* (on its eighth edition in 2015). Knowles argued that if we teach adults in the same way as we teach children/young people then they will be missing out on something. Let us look at four underlying assumptions that Knowles originally made when arguing the differences between andragogy and pedagogy:

1 changes in self-concept
2 the role of experience
3 readiness to learn
4 orientation to learning.

We cannot afford to ignore the fact that adult learners are different from children and young people; if we ignore the differences then there is a chance we will alienate our participants and they will not get the most from the training. However, this does not mean that the whole approach of teaching (or training) needs to be radically different between adults and children/ young people. As well as looking at how these assumptions can affect adult learning, we should ask what lessons we can learn if we apply them to children's learning. Table 12.3 offers a suite of ideas and suggestions.

So, we believe that the underlying assumptions of andragogy listed by Knowles are really important to digest and understand, and it is true that the implications, if we get these wrong, may be more serious for adults than for children/young people. However, when we look at Table 12.3, we can see that the assumptions made by Knowles to improve adult learning can actually begin to have a direct improvement on our school lessons as well.

So, what advice should we give to Nathan, our experienced teacher, when **planning** his first training?

- Start by planning your learning aims – these should be based on the needs for the whole group with an effort also being made to meet individual needs (see Snapshot B, page 33).
- Build some form of assessment into the training (see Chapter 11).
- You need to be ruthless to get rid of activities that are not efficient, engaging or of direct relevance to the participants.

What advice should we give to Nathan when **delivering** his training?

- Show humility; do not patronise the participants, but respect their existing knowledge and experience.
- Be responsive to participant questions and use a variety of interactive activities.
- Do not try to just be an entertainer. There is a time and a place for motivational talks and 'fun', but during training participants should be purposefully active ('engaged'), with some form of assessment.

Table 12.3 How lessons learned from adult training can improve classroom teaching

1 Changes in self-concept

As we become adults we become increasingly self-directing, with an increasing ability (and desire) to choose what we do and how we do it.

Lessons for the adult learner

If we give adults no choice in selecting what courses they attend, or if they are given no choice in the activities they engage in on the courses selected, then they are likely to resist them.

Lessons for the classroom

We are more likely to get 'buy-in', engagement and ultimately concentration from students if we give them some choice. This could be, for example, by letting KS4 (14-16 years old) students choose from a selection of differentiated tasks or by giving pupils in the EYFS (up to the age of five) a free choice of play-based activities.

2 The role of experience

When working with a group of adults, we need to take into account their previous experiences and their possible different starting points. For example, a group of experienced teachers are likely to vary more in their experiences than a cohort of young, initial teacher trainees, who again are likely to vary more than a cross-section of 10-year-old learners.

Lessons for the adult learner

Participant experience provides the scaffolding that any new learning is going to be based around; making links to existing knowledge will 'speed up' the learning and enhance their ability to recall knowledge and strategies. If a trainer acts as if the participants have no experience then they seriously risk patronising or ostracising them.

Lessons for the classroom

Even a handful of six-year-old learners can come with widely different experiences and knowledge. The best lessons we teach will often be ones that encourage students to make links with their existing knowledge and understanding, either at the start, during, or at the end of a lesson (such as SOLO hexagons - see page 168).

3 Readiness to learn

How prepared are we to learn something? In adults this can be triggered by an external event or need, but in children/ young people there is an assumption that once they have reached a level of intellectual maturity there are certain things they should learn that are linked to curriculum content at least.

Lessons for the adult learner

We should think about the order in which we run our training as not every teacher is ready to learn the same thing. Courses like Middle-Leader training or the National Professional Qualification for Headship (NPQH) rely on participants being self-selecting when they are 'ready to learn'.

Lessons for the classroom

There are some subjects where there is a particularly large spread of ability, such as mathematics, where some students intuitively understand some concepts at a much earlier stage than others. Where possible, it is important to be able to support all students so that they can 'pace themselves' so that they are not held back or struggle.

4 Orientation to learning

Whilst it is assumed that most children/young people are happy that they go to school to learn, most adults need to be able to see clearly that the course content will be of use to them personally or in their ability to do their job.

Lessons for the adult learner

Whilst most participants on a course are not expecting every word they hear to be indispensable, they will have a short patience threshold if you are spending too much time on something that is perceived as being irrelevant. You can be honest with participants about why you have structured your training in a particular way if it is not at first obvious how it will help them to solve a particular problem they have.

Lessons for the classroom

It is good practice to consider real-life applications wherever possible. Learning for learning's sake can be very interesting to some students, but generally our lessons will be more engaging if we can make as many links as we can to student-applicable situations.

Finally, what advice can we give Nathan's school when **organising** and **advertising** the training?

As teachers we have frequently found ourselves to be in the middle of the dichotomy of training: everyone wants it but no-one has time for it! Allowing time for quality staff development is frequently heralded as being crucial to a successful school, but it has to be balanced with external pressures on staff due to the cost of training and cover, as well as the internal pressures if teachers have to plan too many cover lessons and then feel they have to 'catch up' with lessons lost. The first trick, when designing a training course, is to ensure it has appeal to both the school and the individual teachers if it is going to recruit well – see Table 12.4 for examples:

Table 12.4 Combining school needs with the individual teacher needs (adapted from the Science Learning Centres, 2011)

Individual needs/priorities	School needs/priorities
Subject knowledge and pedagogy	Ofsted action plan
Basic teaching skills	School development plan
Confidence/motivation/self esteem	League table positions
Doing the job (exam moderation, etc.)	Government priorities
Career enhancement	Legal requirement (such as health and safety)
General interest	Addressing a gap in teaching skills
	LA/Academy chain priorities

Rationale

Learning aims

We have worked with numerous educational organisations and universities, and all have at one time or another suffered with low recruitment on training courses, even after the need has first been identified. There are a range of timings of the training that we can use that will suit some groups of teachers more than others (as explored in Table 12.5).

Table 12.5 Different timings for training sessions and their relative advantages and disadvantages

		Advantages (+)/disadvantages (−) to the school	Advantages(+)/disadvantages (−) to the teacher
One-off events	**Single day** (around 9:15–15:45)	+ This is the 'expected training day', which makes booking cover straightforwards. + Minimises travel times compared to the training time. − Relatively high cover costs.	+ A whole day out can give teachers a 'break' from the day job. − Teachers have to prepare a whole day's cover work.
	Single half-day (around 8:45–11:45 or 13:00–16:00)	+ Reduces cover costs compared to a whole day. − Limited contact time with participants.	+ Often suits support staff really well. + Afternoon sessions can avoid rush-hour traffic. − Participants who have worked hard in the morning may be tired.
	Single twilight (around 15:45–17:15)	+ Works very well for whole departments or whole school training events that are being run in-school. + Will suit schools with tight budgets. − The impact of the training on participants may be minimal (see Chapter 12, pages 182–5).	+ Suits the specific needs of teachers (such as *Successful Revision Techniques*). − Unlikely to attract teachers from schools in rural locations because of the travel time.
	Delayed start (around 13:00–18:00)	+ Get almost a whole day's training with minimal cover costs. − Training may need to take place in spaces already dedicated to after-school/evening classes.	+ A lot of training but teachers will not have to miss too many lessons/write too much cover lessons. − Can be tiring for participants. − Can be awkward for teachers with family commitments.
	Evening (around 17:00–20:30)	+ No cover costs. − Price will need to include the cost of a nice meal and possibly an external venue.	+ Suits 'optional extra' training courses, e.g. those that are not deemed essential but look really interesting. − May not suit teachers with family/evening commitments.
	Conference	+ Works well on Professional Development days as the pressures and costs of setting cover disappear. + Promotes opportunities for networking. − Impact from individual sessions may be minimal (but a few good ideas or contacts may make it worthwhile).	+ Attracts teachers with a general interest in the subject as well as those that have specific needs. − Lacks intimacy, because the trainer cannot get to know the participants well.

Table 12.5 Continued

		Advantages (+)/disadvantages (−) to the school	Advantages(+)/disadvantages (−) to the teacher
Multi-day events	Termly (or twice termly) series with gap-tasks	+ High chance of impact on students (see Chapter 12, pages 182–5). + Improved chance of independent learning. − Gap tasks may consume valuable learning and teaching time.	+ Suits ambitious teachers that are looking to make, and want to be able to demonstrate, progress. − May require a lot of cover lessons to be written. − If participants have to travel, those attending a series of twilights may well have to spend more time travelling than actually participating; as such, most teachers would prefer to have a whole day.
	Longer series (around a fortnight or more)	+ A real need has to be identified. For example, if you do not have a physics teacher you may wish to re-train one of your existing teachers. − The potential for very high cover costs.	+ Can be a massive step up in confidence and abilities to teach a subject. − Can be a very intense and draining experience.
	Weekends/ holidays	+ Very attractive to the school because of zero cover implications. − School building has to be opened which adds to the operational costs.	− Training topic has to have significant appeal to teachers to either suit their needs or their ambitions.

References

Holmes, G. and Abington-Cooper, M. (2000). *Pedagogy vs. Andragogy: A False Dichotomy?* Available at: https://scholar.lib.vt.edu/ejournals/JOTS/Summer-Fall-2000/holmes.html (accessed 3 January, 2017).

Knowles, M. (1973). *The Adult Learner.* Houston: Gulf Publishing Company.

National Science Learning Centres (2011). *Leading Effective Professional Development* [Presentation].

GLOSSARY

This book assumes there will often be a professional context to the training. However, nearly all of the theory and activities are equally applicable to training that is delivered for personal reasons.

Activities
Anything that can be used to energise participants, or to teach, assess or embed the required knowledge, skills or understanding of an idea, strategy or concept.

Aims
The reasons for doing the training in the first place. The number of aims you have and the level of detail in your aims will depend upon your training situation.

Assessment
An activity that provides feedback on the participants' progress to the trainer and or the participants themselves.

Formative assessment
An assessment activity which is designed to provide feedback to the participants and trainer that will result in an improvement in learning.

Getting ready to learn (GRTL)
The early activities that are designed to get participants settled and thinking about how the training can have an impact on them.

Getting to know you (GTKY)
The early activities to ensure that participants know each other and feel comfortable working with one another. Also, an opportunity for the trainer and participants to build a trusting relationship.

Learning space
Sometimes a dedicated training room (or classroom), but at other times it may an ordinary room, a corridor or even a picnic bench.

Main (activity)
The 'bulk' of your training sessions where you run most of the activities in the training.

Participant
Any adult who is going to be receiving training. They may be on the training through choice or because they have been pressured/told to attend.

Plenary	Usually the last part of a training session. Generally used to assess or embed the knowledge/understanding.
Reflection	The process of asking oneself questions to aid learning and inform future actions.
Session	A single piece of training; either as a one-off or as a part of a bigger programme.
Starter	Used at the start of a training session, often to establish existing knowledge.
Summative assessment	An assessment activity which is designed to make an end-of-session or end-of-course assessment of the participants' learning.
Teach, train (vb)	Used interchangeably to indicate the process of transferring knowledge, understanding, skills and attitudes from trainer to participants.
Teaching chain	A set of thematically linked activities that show or encourage progression, either by increasing the level of difficulty or by increasing the participants' independence.
Trainer	You, the reader, or anyone who runs or is planning to run training. The trainer acts as a facilitator of learning rather than just a lecturer (see Chapter 9, Independent learning).
Training (n)/training course	This may be anything from a 30-minute slot on a single day to a regular programme of events that run over a year or longer.

INDEX